The Italian Americans

The Italian Americans

A Multicultural View

Francis N. Elmi, Louis J. Gesualdi,
and Lisa Kuan

Hamilton Books

Lanham • Boulder • New York • Toronto • London

Published by Hamilton Books
An imprint of The Rowman & Littlefield Publishing Group, Inc.
4501 Forbes Boulevard, Suite 200, Lanham, Maryland 20706
Hamilton Books Acquisitions Department (301) 459-3366

6 Tinworth Street, London SE11 5AL, United Kingdom

British Library Cataloguing in Publication Information Available

Library of Congress Control Number: 2020934499

ISBN 978-0-7618-7198-9 (pbk. : alk paper)
ISBN 978-0-7618-7199-6 (electronic)

∞™ The paper used in this publication meets the minimum requirements of American National Standard for Information Sciences Permanence of Paper for Printed Library Materials, ANSI/NISO Z39.48-1992.

This book is dedicated to the approximately 600,000 Italian immigrants in the United States from 1941 to 1942 who were unfairly and unjustly classified as alien enemies.

Contents

Preface

In 2014 The American Italian Sociohistorical Association (AISA) was formed to disseminate information on the Italian American sociohistorical experience including the oppression, exploitation and discrimination of this group in the United States, past and present. In order to disseminate such information, the Association has sponsored four conferences that were held at St. John's University and two international conferences (one in Rome, Italy and one in Cork, Ireland). Moreover, the AISA has formed the American Italian Sociohistorical Association Book series to sponsor the publication of books on the Italian American Experience. This book, *The Italian Americans: A Multicultural View* authored by Francis N. Elmi, Louis J. Gesualdi and Lisa Kuan, is the first book of this series. The book contains eleven papers (chapters). Nine were previously unpublished papers and two chapters were previously published. The chapters of the book that were previously published are "A Brief Discussion on Roseto"[1] and "Popularly Held Beliefs about Italian Americans and Organized Crime."[2]

There have been many misperceptions written about Italian Americans. The purpose of this book is to present research that shows these misperceptions are inaccurate. Also, the purpose of this book is to present information to help the reader become more cognizant of the Italian American experience. It is our wish that this book will stimulate a desire by the reader to become more interested in ethnic studies.

Francis N. Elmi, Louis J. Gesualdi and Lisa Kuan

NOTES

1. This chapter is an updated version of Louis Gesualdi, *The Italian/American Experience: A Collection of Writings* (Lanham, Maryland: University Press of America, 2012). Also, parts of this chapter were presented in Louis Gesualdi, "Closing Remarks" *The Italian American Experience: A Sociohistorical Examination,* American Italian Sociohistorical Association First Conference Series held at St. John's University, Queens, New York (October 21, 2015).

2. This chapter was originally published in Louis Gesualdi, *The Italian American Experience: A Collection of Writings* (Lanham, Maryland: University Press of America, 2012). Also parts of this chapter were presented in Louis Gesualdi "Opening Remarks" and "Closing Remarks," *A Sociohistorical Assessment of Italian American: 1890 to the Present,* American Italian Sociohistorical Association Second Conference Series held at St. John's University, Rome, Italy (June 16, 2016).

Acknowledgments

We wish to thank Katia Passerini, Dean of the Lesley H. and William L. Collins College of Professional Studies, St. John's University, for her support and assistance that enabled us to write this book. Second, we would like to indicate our gratitude to Joseph Scelsa, President and Founder of the Italian American Museum, for his many suggestions and advice over the years. Third, we are very grateful to Elana Pirov, secretary of the Division of Health and Human Services, Lesley H. and William L. Collins College of Professional Studies, St. John's University, for all the help that she has given the American Italian Sociohistorical Association in the last five years. Fourth, we wish to thank Julia A. Varvaro, Graduate Assistant, Lesley H. and William L. Collins College of Professional Studies, St. John's University, for formatting our book and for her assistance. Finally, we wish to acknowledge the assistance of the Hershey, Pennsylvania Archives in providing access to material important to research.

Introduction

It is important that Italian Americans (as well as other groups) are familiar with their own group's experience and to grasp what is considered productive and practical to shaping their lives. The collection of writings (two of the eleven were previously published) chosen for the first American Italian Sociohistorical Association Book Series publication, we hope will be a meaningful beginning for Italian Americans to become informed of their group's experience especially the prejudice and discrimination that Italian Americans experienced in the United States, past and present. This publication contains chapters (works) showing how popular negative notions of Italian American life are inaccurate. Moreover, it contains chapters (writings) that provide useful information on Italian American heritage.

The first chapter "A Brief Look at Some Beccarian Principles" was written by Louis J. Gesualdi and Lisa Kuan. This chapter takes a brief look at some of Beccaria's principles (as discussed in his book ON CRIMES AND PUNISHMENTS) and their influence on the American Constitution, the Bill of Rights and the classical school of criminology.

Second, "A Brief Timeline of the Oppression, Exploitation and Discrimination of Italian Americans in the United States" was written by Louis J. Gesualdi and Lisa Kuan. This chapter presents a brief listing of the oppression, exploitation and discrimination that Italian Americans experienced in the United States, past and present.

Third, "A Comparison of the Italian and Black Sociohistorical Experiences in the United States from 1870 to the Present" was written by Louis J. Gesualdi. This chapter compares the Italian American and African American sociohistorical experiences in the United States from 1870 to the present. Specifically, it presents a bulleted list that point outs the similarities of the experiences of these two groups.

Fourth, "Struggle and Triumph: A History of Prominent Hershey Italian Americans" was written by Francis N. Elmi. The focus of this chapter is to examine the struggles and ultimate success of seven prominent Hershey Italian Americans including an immigrant and six children of immigrants. Because of family connections as well as career similarities in the workplace, six of these individuals created a network of success in Hershey, and in the case of the other individual, she found success in academic renown as an anthropologist and professor far away from Hershey. These 7 prominent individuals had important similarities despite some differences.

Fifth, "The Effect of Fascist Political Repression and the Manifesto of Race on Selected Prominent Italian and Italian American Jewish Academics: Murder and Flight—Italy's Loss and America's Gain—A Multicultural Narrative" was written by Francis N. Elmi. There are many historical examples of the oppression of different cultures in many countries. One notorious example is Fascist Italy's maltreatment of Italian Jews exemplified specifically in this chapter in the lives and careers of Italian Jewish academics and scientists: the Rosselli brothers, Salvador Luria, and Rita Levi-Montalcini. The famed scientist Enrico Fermi was not Jewish but was married to Laura Capon, an Italian Jew. He and his wife escaped persecution by leaving Italy before the Racial Laws had much of an impact. The fate of the Rosselli brothers, Carlo and Nello, both academics and scholars, was tragic. By contrast, Fermi, Luria, and Levi-Montalcini entered the successful multicultural society of mid-twentieth century America.

Sixth, "The Holocaust and Italy" is written by Louis J. Gesualdi and Lisa Kuan. Many people and textbooks have discussed the atrocities that the Jews have faced during WWII and Holocaust but few discuss the triumphs and the kindness of humanity during these times. In this chapter, Gesualdi and Kuan discuss just that. This chapter also discusses Walter Wolff's book *Bad Times Good People: A Holocaust Survivor Recounts His Life in Italy during WWII* and Elizabeth Bettina's book *It Happened in Italy: Untold Stories of How the People Defied the Horrors of the Holocaust.*

Seventh, "A Brief Discussion on Roseto" was written by J. Louis Gesualdi. This chapter discusses John G. Bruhn and Stewart Wolf's *The Roseto Story: An Anatomy of Health* (1979). Bruhn and Wolf's study (sixteen years of research beginning in the early 1960s) investigates the Italian community of Roseto, Pennsylvania. The book's findings indicate that a close knit community (such as the Italian-American community of Roseto) acts as an area of defense against the effects of stress, bereavement and life changes.

Eighth, "Popular Held Beliefs about Italian Americans and Organized Crime" was written by Louis J. Gesualdi. This chapter demonstrates that the commonly held beliefs about Italian Americans and organized crime are not true. It presents social scientific studies indicating that Italian Americans did not develop organized crime in the United States.

Ninth, "A Brief Critique on the 2015 PBS Special on Italian Americans' was written by Lisa Kuan and Louis J. Gesualdi. This chapter presents a brief critique on the 2015 PBS special on Italian Americans. Kuan and Gesualdi's response of the PBS special on the Italian American experience criticizes its presentation of Italian Americans on two general counts. First, there were insufficiencies in the special's description of Italian Americans living in the United States during the last 120 years and second, there were weaknesses in its analysis of the true Italian American experience.

Tenth, "Criticisms of the Banning of Columbus Day" was written by Francis N. Elmi and Louis J. Gesualdi. This chapter presents criticisms of Brown University's banning of Columbus Day.

Eleventh, "Some Ideas for Research and Projects for the American Italian Sociohistorical Association" was written by Louis J. Gesualdi and Lisa Kuan. This chapter offers different ideas for research and projects for the newly formed American Italian Sociohistorical Association.

These eleven chapters are an introduction to an understanding of the sociohistorical experience of Italian Americans, past and present. It is these authors' wish that this publication will stimulate a desire by the reader to become more interested in becoming knowledgeable of the ethnic group experience in the United States.

ONE

A Brief Look at Some Beccarian Principles

Louis J. Gesualdi and Lisa Kuan

Cesare Beccaria, a nobleman, was born in Milan in 1738 and died 1794. In 1764 Beccaria published his famous book ON CRIMES AND PUNISH-MENTS.[1] His book advocated the prevention of crime rather than punishment, and promptness in punishment where punishment was inevitable: above all, it condemned confiscation, capital punishment and torture.[2] Moreover, his book influenced the founding fathers of the United States, especially John Adams. Many of the ideals of the United States were first discussed in Beccaria's work.[3] Furthermore, Cesare Beccaria's principles were influential in the development of the classical school of criminal justice. The classical school is characterized by an emphasis on free will choices, a concern with the way in which government deals with its citizens, and a concern for the basic rights of all people.[4] This chapter takes a brief look at some of Beccaria's principles (as discussed in his book) and their influence on the American Constitution, the Bill of Rights and the classical school of criminology.[5] Listed below are some of these Beccarian principles.

- Laws ought to be conventions among men in a state of freedom and have one end in view: the greatest happiness of the greatest number.
- Every act of authority of one man over another, for which there is no absolute necessity, is tyrannical.
- If men are bound to society, society is equally bound to them.
- In any government, power is vested in the whole of the people and not in any part of the society.

5

- The press makes the people, and not just a few individuals, the guardians and defenders of the laws.
- Members of society have the right to do anything they please provided it is not contrary to the laws—without fearing reprisals of any kind.
- It is an admirable law which ordains that every individual shall be tried by his peers, and that individuals are innocent until found guilty.
- Punishment of a nobleman should not differ from that of the lowest member of society.
- A fundamental principle of legislation is the art of conducting men to maximum happiness and to minimum misery.[6]

These particular Beccarian Principles had a large and lasting impact on the American Constitution and the Bill of Rights, especially their influence to the following amendments to the constitutions: Amendment I (freedom of the press), Amendment V (rights in criminal cases), Amendment VI (rights to fair trial), and Amendment VIII (bails, fines and punishments).[7] Furthermore, Beccaria is remembered today as a founder of the classical school of criminology and as a champion of the cause for humanity. Specifically, some major concepts of the classical school derived from the above Beccarian Principles are utilitarianism (the greatest good for the greatest number); civil rights and due process of law.[8]

Cesare Beccaria's *An Essay on Crimes and Punishments* is a great piece in the democratic tradition. It is a testament to human freedom and social justice. This book is an excellent account of some of the fundamental principles of democratic society and jurisprudence.

American History teachers and professors need to have access to resources that document the Italian and Italian American experiences in American history. Children—and adults—of all nationalities need to know about Cesare Beccaria and many other Italians and Italian Americans who have contributed to America. Teachers and students need to know about the Italian immigrants who helped build America. More importantly, Italian American children need to learn about the accomplishments of Italians and Italian Americans in American history.

In conclusion, because of Beccaria's influence on the American Constitution, Bill of Rights and the classical school of criminal justice, many of the members of the American Italian Sociohistorical Association argue that the name of the John Jay College of Criminal Justice of City University of New York needs to be renamed either Cesare Beccaria College of the City University of New York or at the very least to John Jay/Cesare Beccaria College of the City University of New York.

NOTES

1. See Frank P. Williams III and Marilyn D. McShane, *Criminological Theory,* Englewood Cliffs, NJ: Prentice Hall, 1988: 12–17 and Cesare Beccaria, *An Essay on Crimes and Punishments,* Wellesley, MA: International Pocket Library, 1983.

2. See Cesare Beccaria, *An Essay on Crimes and Punishments,* Wellesley, MA: International Pocket Library, 1983.

3. See Marcello T. Maestro, *Cesare Beccaria and the Origins of Penal Reform.* Philadelphia ,PA: Temple University Press, 1973, Elio D. Monachesi, "Cesare Beccaria," Journal of Criminal Law, Criminology and Political Science 46: 439–49, Marcello T. Maestro, *Voltaire and Beccaria as Reformers of Criminal Law.* New York: Columbia University Press, 1942 and Coleman Phillipson, *Three Criminal Law Reformers: Beccaria, Bentham and Romilly.* Montclair, NJ: Patterson Smith, 1923.

4. Ibid. Also see Frank P. Williams III and Marilyn D. McShane, *Criminological Theory,* Englewood Cliffs, NJ: Prentice Hall, 1988.

5. Originally presented by Louis Gesualdi and Lisa Kuan as a paper "Cesare Beccaria's *On Crime and Punishment: A Preliminary Report,"* Over Five Centuries of Italian American History, American Italian Sociohistorical Association Third Conference Series held at the University of Cork, Cork, Ireland, July 28, 2017.

6. See Cesare Beccaria, *An Essay on Crimes and Punishments,* Wellesley, MA: International Pocket Library, 1983: Back Cover.

7. See Marcello T. Maestro, *Cesare Beccaria and the Origins of Penal Reform.* Philadelphia ,PA: Temple University Press, 1973, Elio D. Monachesi, "Cesare Beccaria," Journal of Criminal Law, Criminology and Political Science 46: 439–49, Marcello T. Maestro, *Voltaire and Beccaria as Reformers of Criminal Law.* New York: Columbia University Press, 1942 and Coleman Phillipson, *Three Criminal Law Reformers: Beccaria, Bentham and Romilly.* Montclair, NJ: Patterson Smith, 1923. Also, see *The Constitution of the United States of America,* New York: American Civil Liberties Union.

8. Ibid. Also, see Frank P. Williams III and Marilyn D. McShane, *Criminological Theory,* Englewood Cliffs, NJ: Prentice Hall, 1988.

TWO

A Brief Timeline of the Oppression, Exploitation, and Discrimination of Italian Americans in the United States

Louis J. Gesualdi and Lisa Kuan

In order to understand the Italian American experience we need to have a better grasp of their historical and current situation in the United States. To help develop this understanding, this chapter presents a brief timeline of the oppression, exploitation and discrimination that Italian Americans experienced in the United States, past and present.[1]

- 1870–1920: 4 million Italians (80 percent from Southern Italy and mostly unskilled labor) migrated to the United States. This was an average of about 100,000 Italians a year coming to the U.S. Most of these immigrants were poor and working at jobs in the U.S. for low wages. Many of these immigrants experienced oppression, while most experienced exploitation and discrimination.[2] 40 percent of these immigrants returned to Italy before 1920[3] and many of them returned due to the negative experience listed above.
- 1870–1920: The majority of Italian immigrants came to work in the United States as unskilled laborers in construction. Many Italian immigrants (numbering hundreds of thousands) came and worked under the harsh conditions of the padrone system. In many cases, these immigrants worked in mines, railroads, agribusiness, and quarries for companies under extremely harsh and unsanitary conditions and for very low wages.[4]
- 1880–1910: Italian Americans in Bridgeport, CT and in other cities of Connecticut had great difficulty getting factory jobs because of

prejudice and discrimination against this group. This can be seen in a newspaper article from *The New Britain Daily Herald* entitled "Down on Foreigners," dated April 3rd, 1903 which reported that many Italian immigrants had experienced harsh prejudice and discrimination at a Southington factory. According to the article, the workers of this factory stated that they had never worked with Italian immigrants and that they would not work with Italians in the future. On the rare occasion that the superintendent in Southington, CT attempted to hire an Italian, the workers of this factory would show their resentment by refusing to work. Therefore, no Italian had been able to work in factories such as this during the early 1900s.[5]

- 1880–1929: For almost fifty years the Italian American Catholics were discriminated against in the American Catholic Church. Because of the political situation after 1870 in Italy resulting from the seizure of the Papal States, there existed a great bitterness between the Italian government and the Church. Italian American Catholics were being punished by the Irish American Catholic clergy for the pro-state attitude held by Italians in the church-state conflict in Italy. Italian Americans had to practice their Catholicism in the basements of the Catholic churches throughout the country. Catholic schools in the United States refused to teach the Italian language until 1929, when Mussolini finally ended the church-state hostility by negotiating the Lateran Treaty with the Vatican.[6]

- 1880 to World War II: Italian Americans were one of the poorest groups living in American cities.[7]

- 1890: The Morgagni Medical Society was founded in New York City as an organization to foster the professional, intellectual and economic development of Italian American physicians who were struggling to establish themselves in an unfriendly and unwelcoming environment for the descendants of new immigrants to the United States at the turn of the nineteenth century.[8]

- March 14, 1891: In New Orleans 11 Italian Americans who were found not guilty of murdering the police chief were lynched by a mob of 8000 individuals in the city. This was the largest lynching in one day in the history of the U.S.[9] A major part of the American press agreed and supported this lynching (including the *New York Times*). Also, even though there was no evidence that showed these 11 Italian Americans being part of the Mafia, they were accused of being members of that criminal organization. This was the beginning of a large contingent of the American press popularizing and stereotyping Italian Americans as members of the Mafia.[10]

- 1900 to the present: There were hundreds, if not thousands of mutual benefit societies created by Italian immigrants throughout the United States to fight discrimination.[11] Other organizations set up by Italian Americans to fight against discrimination against their group include the Sons of Italy, Unico National, the American Italian Historical Association, the John D. Calandra Institute of City University of New York, One Voice, the American Italian Sociohistorical Association and others.

- 1920s: By this decade, Italians were the largest immigrant group to enter the U.S. More than 4 million Italian immigrants had come to this country. As an outcome of this large number of Italian immigrants, anti-Italian sentiment grew. Italians were considered as subhuman and undesirable by many Americans, and employers often refused to hire people of Italian extraction.[12]

- 1920s and 1930s: Yale University School had set up a quota for the number of Jews and Italian Catholics who were to be accepted to its medical school. During this time period, Milton Winternitz was the Dean of Yale's Medical School. His instructions were extraordinarily precise: "Never admit more than five Jews, take only two Italian Catholics, and take no blacks at all."[13]

- 1924: Anti-Italian sentiment by many Americans was a major reason for the passing of the immigration act of 1924. The immigration act of 1924 discriminated against Italian immigrants coming to the U.S. From as high as 200,000 Italians migrating to the U.S. a year from 1880 to 1920, a quota was set of only allowing approximately 4,000 Italian immigrants a year to come to the U.S. because of very strong prejudice against this group Before passage of the immigration act of 1924, 200,000 Italians were permitted to enter the United States a year. However, after the 1924 legislation, a quota was imposed. Only 4,000 per year were permitted to enter.[14] This extreme difference indicated virulent prejudice against Italian immigrants on the part of the American government.

- 1928–1999: 74 percent of all movie films involving Italian American characters negatively portray this ethnic group. This group tends to be portrayed as either criminals or other social undesirables. Most films today with Italian American characters still portray Italian Americans for the most part negatively.[15]

- 1929–1939: Many Americans expressed very strong negative attitudes and/or feelings toward Italians during the Great Depression. For instance, in 1939 a public opinion poll revealed that 50 percent of the respondents believed Italian Americans to be the worst citizens of all immigrants.[16]

- 1941–1942: Approximately 600,000 Italian immigrants who were not American citizens were unfairly and unjustly classified as alien enemies. The government punished these Italian immigrants by pushing them out of their homes, by arresting them, by having curfews imposed, by having their belongings confiscated by law enforcement and by the government using mass surveillance against them. Hundreds of Italian immigrants were also unjustly placed in camps.[17]

- 1976: As a result of statistics gathered in several studies, the City University of New York attempted to address discrimination against Italian Americans by classifying them as an affirmative action group within the university.[18]

- 1979: The John D. Calandra Institute was created within the City University of New York to study concerns of the Italian American community and focus on social justice. One of those concerns was addressing discrimination against this ethnic group at City University of New York.[19]

- 1979 to the present: The Italian American workforce at City University of New York continues to be the most underemployed affirmative action population with no major growth since 1978, while the other affirmative action, racially protected population doubled and tripled.[20]

- 1991 to 2001: In 1991 the National Public Opinion Research for Commission for Social Justice Order Sons of Italy in America's study "Americans of Italian Descent: A Study of Public Images, Beliefs and Misperceptions" reports that 74 percent of the U.S. public see Italian Americans associated with organized crime. Richard A. Capozzola's 2001 work *Finalmente: The Truth about Organized Crime* suggests that the media and politicians, by exaggerating the role of Italian Americans in organized crime, have influenced the public's inaccurate and negative perception of this group. This exaggeration includes the belief that Italian Americans developed organized crime in the United States and that a significant percentage of Italian Americans are involved in the Mafia. Data indicate that contrary to popular belief a significant percentage of Italian Americans are not involved in organized crime.[21] Moreover, the 2001 "Zogby International's National Survey": American Teenagers and Stereotyping reveals that teens learn the less admirable aspects of their heritage from entertainment industry stereotyping. The Report indicates that 46 percent of Italian American teens said that television's portrayal of Italian Americans as crime bosses is accurate and 30 percent said that were proud of their TV image. Also, the report shows that 78 percent of all American teenagers associate Italian Americans with criminal activities.[22]

- Presently: In 2014 The American Italian Sociohistorical Association was formed to disseminate information on the Italian American sociohistorical experience including the oppression, exploitation, and discrimination against this group in the United States, past and present.

- Presently: Media bias still persists. In 2015 the Italic Institute of America, "Film Study 2015 (1914–2014)" found that almost 70 percent of Italian-related films produced from 1914 to 2014 portrayed Italians in a negative light. The Institute also provides a list of more recent media releases that contain negative portrayals of Italians. The list includes cartoons, games, books, television shows, movies and several remakes that turned an unidentified villain into a villain with an Italian surname.[23]

- Presently: A 2015 study of the American History curriculum of public schools found that there were just a few references to Italians and Italian Americans—Christopher Columbus, Giovanni da Verrazzano and Al Capone. Verrazzano had a positive description. However, there were no references to Amerigo Vespucci, John Cabot, Enrico Tonti, Filippo Mazzei, Charles Bonaparte and many other Italians who have contributed to American history. These lack of references demonstrate discrimination against Italian Americans by omission. Furthermore, Columbus was falsely and negatively portrayed as a villain by the American History curriculum. American school curricula examine organized crime in the United States by emphasizing the role of Al Capone rather than including examples of American criminals from all ethnic backgrounds. The curriculum of public school having falsely portrayed Columbus as a villain and discussing "ruthless gangster" Al Capone as Italians who have contributed to American history causes children of Italian background embarrassment and gives them good reason to detach themselves from their culture. To children of other ethnic backgrounds, these teachings display a nonexistence of positive opinion for Italian culture.[24] The 2015 study also indicated that the handling of Spanish explorers, as described by the curriculum, advances questions of objectivity toward Columbus. The four Spanish explorers revealed—Cortes, de Coronado, de Soto and Pizarro—sought gold, either slaughtered and/or made the Native Americans slaves, and seized land. These explorers, however, are defined as determined, brave, clever, and bold, without the negative commentary, without the analysis, and without the criticisms given to Columbus. One wonders if this is due to Columbus's Italian ethnicity.[25]

- Presently: Italian Americans are still viewed stereotypically as gangsters and/or as undesirables.[26] For example, the front cover of the *New York Post* August 14, 2019 entitled GODBOTHER portrays Mario Cuomo, Andrew Cuomo, and Chris Cuomo as gangsters from the Godfather movie.[27] Furthermore, movies still stereotypically portray Italian Americans as gangsters or undesirables. For instance, recently, the 2018 movie "The Green Book" portrays the Italian American character as being crude, violent and buffoonish.[28] In addition, in an upcoming 2020 movie film "The Many Saints of Newark" is a prequel to the TV show "The Sopranos' which portrayed Italian Americans as gangsters and buffoons.[29]

- Presently: There may be as high 1,500 Italian Americans involved in organized crime today and at the most there were as many as 5,000 Italian Americans involved in organized crime from the 1920s to the 1940s at the peak of this group's involvement.[30] It needs to be stated that today the Association of Italian American Educators (AIAE) indicates that there exist over 600,000 Italian American educators in the United States.[31] Now, if we take the peak years of Italian Americans involved in organized crime (5, 000,) and compare that with the number of Italian American educators (over 600,000), one can see a ratio of 120 educators to 1 gangster. Yet in the over one hundred years of movies and over seventy years of TV, look at all the movies and all the documentaries on Italian American gangsters and yet hardly any, if any, movies and documentaries depicting Italian Americans educators. By not presenting Italian American educators, the media exemplified discrimination by omission. By minimizing the role of Italian American educators in film, television shows, or documentaries, the media gives the impression that there are no Italian American teachers, professors, scientists, or writers.

It is important that Italian Americans (as well as other groups) are familiar with their own group's experience and to grasp what is considered productive and practical in shaping their lives. This brief timeline of the oppression, exploitation, and discrimination that Italian Americans experienced in the United States, past and present will hopefully be a meaningful beginning for Italian Americans to become more informed about their own group's experience. Not having knowledge of one's own group's experience (in the case of the Italian Americans) may give the impression that Italian Americans have never experienced oppression, exploitation and discrimination in the U.S. past and present, and that all negative portrayals of Italian Americans by the media and certain politicians are accurate. Also, if members of an ethnic or racial group remain unaware, they may fall victim to oppression, exploitation, and discrimination.

It is important to be aware of our ethnic heritage and emphasize what is positive and productive in doing so. Italian Americans and other ethnic and racial groups should negate the stereotypes in understanding their great contributions to society and understanding the struggles other groups have experienced in American society. It is only then we may develop a more accurate understanding of American history which has heretofore neglected to be portrayed comprehensively and objectively.

NOTES

1. Previously an unpublished paper.

2. Louis J. Gesualdi, *The Bad Things You Have Herd About Italian Americans Are Wrong: Essays on Popular Prejudice*, Lewiston, NY: The Edwin Mellen Press, 2014.

3. Ibid. and See the 2015 PBS special on Italian Americans.

4. See Louis J. Gesualdi, *The Italian Immigrants of Connecticut, 1880 to 1940*, New Haven, Connecticut: Connecticut Academy of Arts and Sciences, 1997 and Richard D. Alba, *Italian Americans into the Twilight of Ethnicity*, Englewood Cliffs, New Jersey: Prentice-Hall, Inc., 1985.

5. See Gesualdi, *Italian Immigrants of Connecticut, 1880 to 1940*, pp. 13–29.

6. Richard Gambino, *Blood of Mu Blood: The Dilemma of the Italian-Americans*, New York: Doubleday, 1974.

7. See Louis J. Gesualdi, *Italian Immigrants of Connecticut, 1880 to 1940*.

8. See Morgagni Medical Society of New York, ABOUT Us Page, Morgagnimedicalsociety.com.

9. See Tom Smith, *The Crescent City Lynchings: The Murder of Chief Hennessy, the New Orleans "Mafia" Trials, and the Parish Prison Mob*, Guilford, CT: The Lyons Press, 2007.

10. Ibid.

11. Nathan Glazer and Daniel P. Moynihan, *Beyond the Melting Pot*, Cambridge, Massachusetts: The M.I.T. Press 1970, p. 194.

12. See Eric Blakemore, "Why America Targeted Italian Americans during World War II," History.com, January 19, 2019.

13. Gerard N. Burrow *A History of Yale's School of Medicine: Passing Torches to Others*, New Haven, CT: Yale University Press, 2002.

14. See Alba, *Italian Americans Into the Twilight of Ethnicity*.

15. Louis J. Gesualdi, *The Italian/American Experience: A Collection of Writings*, Lanham, Maryland: University Press of America, 2012.

16. Bruce M. Stave and John F. Sutherland with Aldo Salerno, *From the Old Country: An Oral History of European Migration to America*, New York: Twayne Publishers, 1994, p. xv.

17. Blakemore, "Why America Targeted Italian Americans during World War II," History.com, January 19, 2019 and the 2015 PBS special on Italian Americans.

18. See Italian Americans ONE VOICE Coalition Supports Court Petition to Have Italian Americans Included in CUNY Affirmative Action Plan, May 25, 2018, iaovc.org and Vincenzo Milione (presentation) "Italian American Workforce and Labor Pool Changes" at the Italian Americans and Discrimination in Higher Education Conference held at St. John's University, Queens, NY, March 27, 2013.

19. See Italian Americans ONE VOICE Coalition Supports Court Petition to Have Italian Americans Included in CUNY Affirmative Action Plan, May 25, 2018, iaovc.org.

20. See Italian Americans ONE VOICE Coalition Supports Court Petition to Have Italian Americans Included in CUNY Affirmative Action Plan, May 25, 2018, iaovc.org and Vincenzo Milione (presentation) "Italian American Workforce and Labor Pool Changes" at the Italian Americans and Discrimination in Higher Education Conference held at St. John's University, Queens, NY, March 27, 2013.

21. Louis J. Gesualdi, *The Italian/American Experience: A Collection of Writings*, Lanham, Maryland: University Press of America, 2012.

22. Ibid.

23. Janice Therese Mancuso, "Searching for Italian American History" (paper) presented at the American Italian Sociohistorical Association First Conference Series entitled *The Italian American Experience: A Sociohistorical Examination* held at St. John's University, Queens, NY, October 21, 2015. Also, see Italic Institute of America, "Film Study 2015 (1914–2014)," italic.org/media watch/filmstudy.php, 2015, and see Italic Institute of America , "Exhibit A: Examples of Media Bias,"italic.org/anti_defamation/ExhibitA.php., 2015.

24. Janice Therese Mancuso, "Searching for Italian American History" (paper) presented at the American Italian Sociohistorical Association First Conference Series enti-

tled *The Italian American Experience: A Sociohistorical Examination* held at St. John's University, Queens, NY, October 21, 2015.

25. Ibid.

26. Louis J. Gesualdi, *The Italian/American Experience: A Collection of Writings,* Lanham, Maryland: University Press of America, 2012.

27. See the front cover of the New York Post August 14, 2019.

28. See the 2018 movie "The Green Book"

29. See "The Many Saints of Newark," Movie-MOVIEWEB and the "Sopranos' TV Series 1999–2007–IMDb.

30. Louis J. Gesualdi, *The Italian/American Experience: A Collection of Writings,* Lanham, Maryland: University Press of America, 2012.

31. Carmela Leonardi, "AIAE Association of Italian American Educators 20 Years of Dedication to the Promotion of Italian Language and Culture" (presentation) at the American Italian Sociohistorical Second St. Joseph's Day Celebration Program Conference Series held at St. John's University, Queens, NY, April 4, 2017.

THREE

A Comparison of the Italian and Black Sociohistorical Experiences in the United States from 1870 to the Present

Louis J. Gesualdi

This chapter presents a comparison of the Italian and Black sociohistorical experiences in the United States from 1880 to the present.[1] Below is a bullet list to point out the similarities of the experiences of these two groups.

- Most Italian immigrants (over 80 percent coming from rural Southern Italy) from 1870 to 1920[2] and most African Americans from the Southern U.S. states from 1870 to 1920 came from farming backgrounds.[3] Most of these African Americans were sharecroppers[4] and most of these Italian immigrants were day laborers.[5]
- In the U.S., both worked on the railroads, mines, factories and construction.[6]
- African Americans were the largest group lynched in the U.S. Thousands of African Americans were killed.[7] There were Italian Americans lynched in the U.S. The largest lynching in one day in American history was in New Orleans in 1891 where 11 Italian Americans were lynched.[8]
- From 1870 to 1970 a large percentage of Italian Americans lived in Little Italies of cities throughout the U.S.[9] From 1910 to the present a large percentage of African Americans live in segregated areas of cities throughout the U.S.[10]
- The two groups were two of the poorest groups living in American cities from 1880 to World War II.[11]

- There have been a number of scholars (for instance, Thomas Sowell, Edward C. Banfield, Nathan Glazer and Daniel P. Moynihan) who unfairly claimed that the poverty of Italian and African Americans was the result of their own cultural values.[12]
- The two groups had large numbers of individuals (over 1 million Italian Americans and around one million African Americans) fighting in World War II.[13]
- Both groups have a long history of success in the entertainment industry in the U.S. –especially sports and music.[14]
- Since 1915 the movie industry has a long history of stereotyping Italian Americans and African Americans as criminals, buffoons and/or as other socially undesirables.[15]
- Both groups have had a large number of individuals involved in human rights activism. African Americans had such individuals as M.L. King, Malcolm X and others.[16] Italian Americans had such individuals as Fiorello LaGuardia, Vito Marcantonio and others.[17]
- There exist a hundred years of Italian American scholars involved in Italian American Studies and African American scholars involved in African American studies.[18]
- There is a history of different Italian American organizations and different African American organizations which were developed in response to fight discrimination against their respective groups. For Italian Americans such organizations include the hundreds if not thousands of mutual benefit societies throughout the United States which were created by Italian immigrants.[19] Other organizations set up by Italian Americans include the Sons of Italy,[20] Unico National,[21] the American Italian Historical Association[22] and the John D. Calandra Institute.[23] African Americans set up such organizations as the NAACP, Southern Poverty Law Center, and have organized peaceful demonstrations of the 1950s and 1960s, and others.[24]
- Finally, Italian Americans and African Americans are both affirmative action groups at the City University of New York (CUNY).[25]

In conclusion, one can see that Italian Americans and African Americans have a lot of similarities in their sociohistorical experiences. As one examines the sociohistorical events of these two groups, as well as other groups, one will see that people in general have more in common than they have differences.

NOTES

1. Previously unpublished paper.
2. Richard Alba, *Italian Americans into the Twilight of Ethnicity*, Englewood Cliffs, NJ: Prentice-Hall, 1985.

3. See Thomas N. Mahoney, "African Americans in the Twentieth Century." EH.Net Encyclopedia, edited by Robert Whaples. January 14, 2002 and Stephen Steinberg, *Turning Back: The Retreat from Racial Justice.* Boston, MA: Beacon Press, 1995.

4. See Stephen Steinberg, *Turning Back: The Retreat from Racial Justice.* Boston, MA: Beacon Press, 1995.

5. Joseph Lopreato, *Italian Americans.* New York: Random House, 1970.

6. See Richard Alba, *Italian Americans into the Twilight of Ethnicity,* Englewood Cliffs, NJ Prentice-Hall: 1985 and see Online Encyclopedia: African American History People—www.blackpast.org.

7. Ida B. Well-Barnett, *On Lynchings.* Mineola, NY: Dover Publications, 2014.

8. Tom Smith, *The Crescent City Lynchings: The Murder of Chief Hennessy, the New Orleans Mafia Trials, and the Parish Prison Mob,* Guilford, CT: The Lyons Press, 2007.

9. See Richard Alba, *Italian Americans into the Twilight of Ethnicity,* Englewood Cliffs, NJ: Prentice-Hall, 1985 and Louis J. Gesualdi, *The Italian Immigrants of Connecticut, 1880 to 1940,* New Haven, CT: The Connecticut Academy of Arts and Sciences, 1997.

10. See Algernon Austin, "African Americans Are Still Concentrated in Neighborhoods with High Poverty and Still Lack Full Access to Decent Housing," in www.epi. org/publications/african-americans-concentrated-neighborhoods.

11. See Louis J. Gesualdi, *The Italian Immigrants of Connecticut, 1880 to 1940,* New Haven, CT: The Connecticut Academy of Arts and Sciences, 1997 and Stephen Steinberg, *Turning Back: The Retreat from Racial Justice.* Boston, MA: Beacon Press, 1995.

12. See Louis J. Gesualdi, *The Italian American Experience: A Collection of Writings,* Lanham, Maryland: University Press of America, 2012: 13–25.

13. See Peter L. Belmonte. *Italian Americans in World War II,* Mt. Pleasant, SC: Arcadia Publishing, 2001, Maria Hohn, "African American GIs of WWII: Fighting for Democracy Abroad and at Home" in *Black Military History-Military Times,* militarytimes.com, January 30, 2018, and Christopher Paul Moore, *Fighting for America: Black Soldiers—The Unsung Heroes of World War II,* New York: The Random House Publishing Group, 2005.

14. See Michael Barcella, *Italactors 101 Years of Italian Americans in U.S. Entertainment,* Washington, DC: National Italian American Foundation, 2000 and National Italian American Sports Hall of Fame, www.niashf.org, David K Wiggins, *More Than a Game: A History of the African American Experience in Sport,* New York: Rowman and Littlefield, 2018, and Mellonee V. Burnim and Portia K. Maultsby (editors), *African American Music: An Introduction* (second edition), New York: Taylor and Francis, 2015.

15. See Louis J. Gesualdi, *The Italian American Experience: A Collection of Writings,* Lanham, Maryland: University Press of America, 2012: 27–31 and Cynthia L. Vigliotti, Gianna Vivo, Salvatore Attardo and Sarah Brown-Clark, "Stereotyping Ethnicity: The Ideology of Film Representations of Italian Americans and African Americans" in Dan Ashyk, Fred L. Gardaphe and Anthony Julian Tamburri, *Shades of Black and White: Conflict and Collaboration Between Two Communities,* Staten Island, NY: American Italian Historical Association, 1999: 218–226.

16. Brad Witter, "Martin Luther King Jr. and 8 Black Activists Who Led the Civil Rights Movement," *Biography* in biography.com, June 24, 2019.

17. See Alyn Brodsky, *The Great Mayor: Fiorello LaGuardia and the Making of the City of New York,* New York: Truman Talley Books, 2003 and Gerald Meyer, *Vito Marcantonio: Radical Politician 1902–1954,* Albany, NY: State University of New York Press, 1989.

18. See American Italian Historical Association Proceedings, 1968 to 2005, 50 African Americans Who Forever Changed Academia—OnlineCollege, and Nicki Lisa Cole, "11 Black Scholars and Intellectuals Who Influenced Sociology," in thoughtco.com, July 3, 2019.

19. See Richard Alba, *Italian Americans into the Twilight of Ethnicity,* Englewood Cliffs, NJ: Prentice-Hall, 1985, Joseph Lopreato, *Italian Americans,* New York: Random House, 1970 and Nathan Glazer and Daniel P. Moynihan, *Beyond the Melting Pot,* Cambridge, MA: The M.I.T. Press, 1970.

20. See Order of Sons and Daughters of Italy in America, About Us—osia.org.

21. See UNICO National, About UNICO—www.unico.org.

22. See American Italian Historical Association Proceedings, 1968 to 2005.

23. Joseph Scelsa, "Italian Americans as an Affirmative Action Category at CUNY," paper presented at the *Italian Americans and Discrimination in Higher Education Conference* held at St. John's University, Queens, NY, 2013.

24. See Kenneth R. Janken, "The Civil Rights Movement 1919–1960s, Freedom's Story, TeacherServe. National Humanities Center. December 29, 2019. http://national-humanitiescenter.org/tserve/freedom/1917beyond/essays/crm.htm and Southern Poverty Law Center About Us, http://www.splcenter.org.

25. Vincenzo Milione, "Italian American Workforce and Labor Pool Changes" (presentation) at the *Italian Americans and Discrimination in Higher Education Conference* held at St. John's University, Queens, NY, 2013.

FOUR

Struggle and Triumph

A History of Prominent Hershey Italian Americans

Francis N. Elmi

Growing up in Hershey, Pennsylvania, is a special experience. Hershey has many unusual amenities not ordinarily found in Central Pennsylvania: a castle-like Hotel Hershey on a hill overlooking the town, a Mediterranean-inspired building built by Milton S. Hershey, the lord of Chocolate Town. Could it be that the Italian immigrants, who numbered at one point to approximately 50 percent of the population, felt so comfortable there because, in an ironic way, it reminded them of the medieval atmosphere and social hierarchy of the small so recently feudal villages and towns they left behind in Italy? The Italianate theme seemed to pervade Hershey in the early to mid-twentieth century. In addition to the Hershey Hotel, there was the Hershey Community Building, an Italianate structure on Chocolate Avenue, the main street in town. This building housed the Hershey Junior College, a large dining room for community events, a large well-furnished and well-stocked library, a Little Theatre for small college plays and a large theatre for movies and off Broadway plays. The large theatre has a Pompeian style foyer and entrance hall, lavishly furnished, while over the entrance to the seating area is a gold mosaic ceiling which is a replica of the entrance way ceiling in St. Mark's Cathedral in Venice. In addition the theatre has Venetian style windows and faux balconies. There was also a sports arena and in the past a large swimming pool with sunken gardens as well as the Starlight Ballroom where big bands like Tommy Dorsey and Italian American stars like Frank Sinatra appeared. The ballroom was also the site of political thousand dollars a plate dinners for presidential candidates like Eisenhower and Nixon, Hershey always and seemingly forever a Republican and conservative bastion. Enhancing the Italian atmosphere in downtown Hershey was at one time the famous Cocoa Inn with neo-classic columns reminding many passers-by of Rome, Italy.[1]

All of this was created by the Chocolate King, Mr. Hershey, born a Mennonite who married a Roman Catholic Irish-American wife, Catherine Sweeney in the rectory of St. Patrick's Cathedral in New York.[2] Many Italian Americans who were raised in Hershey often felt estranged from the Mennonites who always seemed so serious and prayerful, while they, by contrast, were more vivacious and fun-loving. This may have made Italian Americans seem foreign and exotic to the conservative Protestants of Central Pennsylvania. It is therefore ironic that a Mennonite with Catholic tastes built an iconic chocolate company and a glamorous town in the middle of the cornfields and farms of rural Pennsylvania over ninety miles from Philadelphia where the Amish lived nearby and time seemed to have stopped. The influx of Italian immigrants as cheap labor transformed the culture and ethos of Hershey, Pennsylvania, as the first group to develop home ownership despite their early poverty. As a result, Hershey became a well-groomed residential town with the best school district in the area even today. And Hershey has always been a magnet for business, entertainment, and education that it still is today and has been almost from its inception in 1903.[3]

According to Natalie Mykta Dekle's overview of the Italian community in Hershey, *Building a New Life: The Italian Community in Hershey.* Italian immigrants who settled in Hershey came primarily from Tuscany, Le Marche, and Abruzzi, thus mainly from Central Italy, although a few families came from the Veneto, Campania, Puglia, Lazio, Calabria, and Sicily.[4]

The focus of this chapter is to examine the struggles and ultimate success of five prominent Hershey Italian Americans including an immigrant and four children of immigrants. Because of family connections as well as career similarities in the workplace, four of these individuals created a network of success in Hershey, and in the case of Lola Romanucci-Ross, she found success in academic renown as an anthropologist and professor far away from Hershey. These prominent individuals had important similarities despite some differences. Angelo Elmi, Edward Tancredi, and Samuel Tancredi's transcripts of their oral histories from the Hershey Community Archive are the major resources for this research. In the case of Alvesta Tancredi, a published interview is the resource, and the source of material in the discussion of Lola Romanucci Ross is her autobiographical text, *To Love the Stranger: The Making of an Anthropologist.*

The literature about the history and society of Hershey focuses mostly on the great success of Milton Snavely Hershey in creating his chocolate and entertainment empire as well as showcasing his progressive and charitable accomplishments. And, of course, it is true that as a philanthropist, he is a role model for corporate executives throughout the United States and the world.[5] However, most of the literature about Hershey, Pennsylvania, does not emphasize the Italian American struggles, successes, and significant contributions of the Italian American immigrants and their descendants. Only in the oral histories from the Hershey Community Archive, the Dekle text, and the D'Antonio biography of M.S. Hershey can we unearth the specific details of their lives and their significance in the story of Hershey, Pennsylvania. For her assistance in providing me with access to the oral histories, I want to thank Tammy Hamilton, the archivist at the Hershey Community Archive who assisted greatly in this endeavor. I also want to thank the Hershey-Derry Township Historical Association and the Hershey Library.

It is the intention of this study to add to Dekle's efforts in contributing to the analysis of Italian American history in Hershey. The contributions of Italian immigrants began very early in the founding of the Hershey chocolate enterprise:

> By spring [1903] fifty workers—all "Italians," according to the Harrisburg paper—were using hand tools, horses, and dynamite to reach the stone substrate that would be the base for construction of a factory that would cover six acres. While this site work was being done, quarrymen [also, mostly Italian] were mining Hershey's own land for the limestone that would be used for outer walls and stone-crunching equipment . . . turning out gravel for roads.[6]

Thus, the very foundation of the famous Hershey Chocolate factory resulted largely from the work of the first generation of Italian immigrants in Hershey.

On the other hand, however, anti-Italian prejudice and discrimination took root in Hershey despite the hard labor the immigrants performed. A striking example occurred when a janitor in a private note to his managers made this statement quoted by D'Antonio in his masterful biography-history, entitled *Hershey: Milton S. Hershey's Extraordinary Life of Wealth, Empire, and Utopian Dreams*. Despite language problems, the newcomers fit well into the factory. But they did meet with prejudice. This took the form of social slights and slanders. Typical was a suggestion note submitted to managers by a company janitor:

> Since many of your employees complain to me that next to their locker is that of an Italian, and because I know very well the conditions of an Italian home having repaired many . . . they contain everything from a bedbug down and all smell like limburger [sic] cheese factory. Therefore I would advise [sic] respectfully that indiscriminate distribution of lockers be abandoned, that foreigners be given their lockers in a contin-

uous [sic] section by themselves. . . . The above frank statement is
exclusively between you the management and me.[7]

It is noteworthy that the writer of this statement wanted it to be confiden-
tial since quite obviously he knew that its contents displayed prejudice,
and he most likely did not want to suffer any consequences from his
hurtful utterance.

In spite of prejudice and early poverty, the Italian Americans gradually adjusted to life in Chocolate Town. Nearly everyone in Hershey, Italian
Americans and non-Italians, admired and loved Mr. Hershey, the Pennsylvania Dutch and the Italians, including the subjects of this study. Perhaps the Italian family structure and their parents' recent experience in
the social structure of Italy where recent feudalism, the papacy, and the
aristocracy prevailed seemed similar to the hierarchical organization of
the Hershey Chocolate enterprise and the town of Hershey itself. The
Italian immigrants felt a familiarity and comfort in life in Hershey.[8]

Angelo Elmi and his parents, for example, like many Italian immigrants in Hershey, were originally from Pitigliano in southern Tuscany
near Rome.[9] The panorama of Pitigliano suggests that of a large castle,
with a series of dwellings, a cathedral and a medieval fortress arising
from a parapet of tufa stone overlooking a valley. One has a sense of
impregnable antiquity. The origins of Pitigliano are prehistoric going
back to the Bronze Age. There are numerous Etruscan tombs nearby as
well as two other ancient towns, Sorano and Sovana. Indeed, there is a
necropolis along the Melata Creek. Few traces are left from the Roman
period although the name of Pitigliano goes back to its historical founding when, according to legend, the Roman families Petilia and Ciliano
stole the gold crown of Jupiter from the Campidoglio, the capitol area in
Rome, and hid it in the tufa stone spur that eventually became Pitigliano.[10]

In the Middle Ages, the Lombardic Aldobrandeschi family conquered
Pitigliano, but in 1274 C.E. Pitigliano became the possession of the Orsini,
a wealthy, prestigious Roman family, as a result of a marriage between
the Orsini nephew of Pope Niccolo IV and Anastasia, the last heir of the
Aldobrandeschi. In the fifteenth century Count Niccolo III of the Orsini
family, who was a descendant of Anastasia Aldobrandeschi., became a
national Italian hero as a result of his military prowess in the service of
many rulers in Italy, including Lorenzo Magnifico of the Medici family in
Florence, the King of Naples, the Pope, and the Doge of Venice. As a
result he was mentioned in Machiavelli's *The Prince.* Later the Medici
ruled Pitigliano, but the city fared badly because Medici power was in
decline, and Pope Urban VIII sought to gain control, and the Medici had
to spend valuable resources in beating back the Papal Army. Pitigliano
became impoverished, but in the 1660s, the situation improved greatly
under the rule of the Dukes of Hapsburg-Lorraine who began disman-

tling the feudal system. The Grand Duke of Tuscany, Leopold II, promoted public works, and in the nineteenth century, the Hapsburg-Lorraine dukes began a cultural academy in literature and the sciences in Pitigliano. By 1860 Pitigliano youth contributed to the battle for the unification of Italy. Pitigliano was annexed to the newly formed Kingdom of Italy.[11]

A positive aspect of life in Pitigliano was the advent of Italian Jews whose presence in the city dates back four centuries when Jews sought refuge in Pitigliano from persecution in the Papal States during the rule of Pope Paul IV in the 1500s; his persecution of Jews in Rome was extreme: "The Jews of Rome were herded into ghettos, forced to sell their property to Christians and made to wear yellow headgear; copies of the Talmud were searched out and burned"; Paul IV also strengthened the Inquisition in Rome.[12] The Jews who fled to Pitigliano built a temple with the Torah. They formed their own schools including the Israelite University and were allowed to buy property and open businesses as artisans. They also formed a library. The Jews lived in a ghetto near the Catholic cathedral but were also permitted to live outside the ghetto. Their high level of literacy influenced the Catholic inhabitants of Pitigliano positively.[13]

Today there are no more Jews in Pitigliano because during World War II they suffered discrimination and danger from German occupation of the city. The Etruscan caves beneath the city became a hiding place for the Jews of Pitigliano, and they were protected and provided food to sustain them by the Catholics until the Germans left. Some became partisans and went north and some left Italy and came to the United States.[14] Some Italian Jews came to Hershey, PA earlier in the twentieth century and it seemed to be common knowledge that they were not allowed to buy property in Hershey.[15]

About the refusal to allow Jews to buy property in Hershey, Lola Romanucci Ross in *To Love the Stranger: The Making of an Anthropologist* stated:

> [Mr. Hershey] wanted no Jews owning property in his town. In those times this was accomplished with ease; but he was not a "racist." His reasoning was as follows: Jews would be unable to resist setting up a store or some sort of industry, therefore he would avert this threat by keeping out those he assumed would always be perpetrators of business enterprise, the non-Jews he could handle.[16]

It is ironic to note that in an ancient Italian city like Pitigliano, Jews were allowed to own property, but in Hershey in the early days of its existence, it seemed to be common knowledge that they could not! Romanucci Ross's use of the word "perpetrators" has a negative connotation suggesting crime. And whether or not the desire of Mr. Hershey to keep Jews out of his town is racist is at least debatable no matter how talented, creative, philanthropic, and good- natured Mr. Hershey surely was.

Currently in Pitigliano, the synagogue has been restored along with the kosher baths and baking ovens and this complex has become a Jewish museum where pilgrims from all over Europe come to visit and the nickname of Pitigliano has become "La Piccola Gerusalemma," little Jerusalem.[17]

Considering the medieval, papal, Medici and ducal history of Pitigliano, it may be that since Angelo Elmi and his family, as stated previously, were originally from Pitigliano, they were accustomed to patriarchal and dictatorial rule, and as time passed they adjusted well and learned how to negotiate the benevolent dictatorship that dominated life in Hershey, Pennsylvania. A great symbol of the almost royal and god-like image Mr. Hershey enjoyed in his town is Founder's Hall, which resembles a quasi-religious monument to the creator of the company and the town. D'Antonio describes this "temple":

> an enormous (some say monstrous) building with a domed rotunda, an auditorium seating 2700 people. The hall was constructed with nearly 1500 tons of Vermont marble and features, according to the school [the Milton S. Hershey School which controls the Trust that owns the Hershey Chocolate enterprise] the second largest domed rotunda in the world. Inside where a fountain gurgles and tourists gawk, a mosaic depicts a dozen key moments in Mr. Hershey's life as if they were the Stations of the Cross. The life-size bronze statue of the founder standing with his arm draped over a boy [originally the school was created to educate and house white orphan boys; now it educates and houses racially diverse boys and girls] greets those who enter the cathedral-like space.[18]

The families of Edward Tancredi and Samuel Tancredi (transcripts of their oral histories from the Hershey Community Archive), Alvesta Tancredi (published interview) and Lola Romanucci Ross (her autobiographical text) also originated in Central Italy in Le Marche near the city of Ascoli Piceno. Like Pitigliano and its environs this region had ancient origins. The Romans conquered Ascoli Piceno in the third century B.C. Later, it was ruled by the Ostrogoths, the Lombards, and the Franks. After 1006 it was ruled by bishops and then became a free municipality but political instability caused it to be ruled by outside dictators which ultimately led to Papal control. In 1860, like Pitigliano, it was annexed with Le Marche and Umbria by the Kingdom of Italy. The history of Ascoli Piceno was a series of dictatorships; thus, the families of Edward Tancredi, Samuel Tancredi, Alvesta Tancredi and the Lola Romanucci Ross, like Angelo Elmi and his family, may have been accustomed to patriarchal rule in Italy and after arriving in Hershey, they had difficulty, but eventually they flourished in the Chocolate Kingdom.[19]

ORAL HISTORY OF ANGELO ELMI

Angelo Elmi was born in Pitigliano, Province of Grosseto in Tuscany on January 18, 1916. In Pitigliano his mother and grandmother took care of him alone because his father was in the Italian Army fighting in World War I against the Austrians for several years. Disillusioned with Italy and tired of poverty and struggle, Francesco Elmi decided to take his family to America in 1920. Angelo sailed to New York at the age of three and a half and arrived at Ellis Island in September of 1920.[20] Upon arriving in Hershey, shortly after Ellis Island, the Elmis lived west of Hershey near the stone quarry and slept in an attic. They had little privacy, for they could see the people next door by candlelight. Angelo indicated that there was no electricity, no running water, and no indoor toilet. Francesco worked for Hershey Chocolate in the factory as a mechanic for the rest of his life.[21]

It took a great deal of courage for the Elmi family to come to America, especially because the Paioletti branch of the family had tried to emigrate in 1915, but their ship, *The Ancona,* was torpedoed by the Germans in the Mediterranean and most of those relatives never had the courage to attempt another voyage to America.[22]

From the attic where they first lived, the Elmis then moved to a hamlet in the northwestern part of Hershey known as Swatara Station, the Little Italy of Hershey at that time. They rented a house; Angelo said it was "terrible."[23] By 1933, they managed to move to West Granada Avenue, which was to become the new Little Italy/Little Pitigliano.

Despite his language difficulties in the early years of his education, Angelo became Valedictorian of the Vocational Technical Program in Hershey High School in 1934. He went on to Hershey Junior College to graduate as the valedictorian there.[24] These educational accomplishments augured well for his outstanding professional career in Hershey.

In remembering his teen-age years, Angelo said, "Man, I worked hard. . . . My parents, they [had] just built their house. Really, I worked a lot."[25] He worked so hard in order to give his mother the money he earned to help pay the mortgage for the house on West Granada Avenue.[26]

Angelo's first job at Hershey was in the wrapping room where the chocolate bars were wrapped in the iconic packaging that has continued until today. Soon afterwards, Angelo's ability and acumen were recognized, and he began working as an electrician. Then he was promoted to increasingly important positions: design draftsman, associate engineer, project engineer, and ultimately project manager.[27] Because of these prominent positions he had at the Hershey factory, Angelo Elmi was involved in the designing and supervising the construction of major facilities for the Hershey Chocolate Corporation and for the town of Hershey; in addition he designed many private homes in Hershey.[28]

At the beginning of his career, the notorious 1937 strike against the Hershey Chocolate enterprise occurred. Angelo described the violence between the strikers and their opposition in this very first strike against the Mr. Hershey's Chocolate Corporation. His description seemed quite general until he said, "There was very much prejudice against the Italians. . . . Until the Second World War, when, as you can see down here [referring to a World War II memorial in Hershey] . .you can see there's Italian names on here. A lot of Italians wounded. Then the Pennsylvania Dutch changed . . . you know how they are . . . unless they know you for ten, twelve, fifteen years, they don't want to associate with you. But now you know, I've been around here so long, they think I'm one of them, and I am. I want to be American."[29]

In reality, he often did not feel that he had been treated fairly—as an Italian American. In the very next statement, after asserting that he had become so American (in the Hershey Archives interview), he says, "I can tell you a couple stories about prejudice, but I don't know if you want to hear them or not."[30] But the interviewer seemed to overlook or neglect this statement.

In his statement about the 1937 strike, Angelo seemed to experience an internal role conflict between being an American company man (part of management) and being loyal to his Italian family worker heritage; "I was right on the wall, either that side or that side [of the strike]. My dad was working inside [Francesco Elmi was in the union and on strike]. You know. I had to watch myself. I felt for the people that worked there, but I didn't want to lose my job. You know, I went so far and no farther."[31] Despite this internal conflict, Angelo moved forward ultimately orchestrating his success at the Hershey Chocolate Corporation.

ORAL HISTORY OF EDWARD C. TANCREDI

Edward Tancredi's oral history records a career parallel to that of his friend and colleague, Angelo Elmi. Edward was born on October 17, 1916, in Hershey ten months after Angelo was born in Italy. Thus Edward had a bit of a head start in America. Edward's father, Antonio Tancredi from near Ascoli Piceno, worked in the quarries as a laborer after working elsewhere in Pennsylvania. When Edward was ten years old the Tancredi family moved to Swatara, the original Little Italy of Hershey. Prior to that they lived next to the railroad tracks:

> We were very close to—maybe my brother [Samuel whose oral history is also the subject of this study] told you the same thing. That's where he was born, as a matter of fact, next to the railroad. When the train

used to go by, you'd be in bed and the old bed used to shake [laughter].[32]

Edward's older sisters, who were quite young when he was born, worked for Hershey to help support the family, one of whom was only eleven when she started working. She died of the Spanish flu when she was only eighteen. She and her sister started working so young because the child labor laws were not yet in effect. Edward's sisters were not expected to obtain much education. Very few young people went to college, and most high school students worked and brought their paychecks home to their parents. Edward's mother, Louisa Romanucci Tancredi, could not read; she could only write her name. But she wanted her children to obtain an education. Eventually, the Tancredis were able to move to Caracas Avenue, a better section of Hershey, one block from West Granada Avenue, where the Elmis were finally able to live in an attractive, quiet neighborhood. Edward remembered Pronio's Italian grocery store as having food that was not packaged, but very fresh. Food was delivered to Italian homes. There were no deadlines to pay for groceries; instead, there was an honor system, an informal line of credit. There was much trust in the Italian immigrant community.

Although Edward indicated that he enjoyed growing up in Hershey, he felt that some people shied away from Italians. He said that he never had a problem, but he then recognized that prejudice still existed in 1991 at the time of this interview for his oral history when he stated:

"Even today [1991] there's a certain amount of prejudice that exists."[33] The interviewer then says "when I got to Hershey, if you weren't Italian, you were a little bit lower. The Italians owned Hershey in 1971."[34]

Edward responded that the Italians in Hershey made sure that they eventually became prosperous enough to become homeowners, but he also said:

> Some of the Italians had difficulty getting ahead because they were Italian, or of Italian descent . . . even today, you say "Ed Tancredi." "Oh yeah. Oh, the Italian." You know I'm no more Italian than you are. I'm Italian by the fact that my parents were Italian, but I was born here and raised in this country. Okay?[35]

Thus, although Edward asserted that he was American, just as Angelo Elmi did, he did also show resentment at the continued, perhaps diminished, problems Italian Americans have had as recently as 1991. And both Edward and Angelo's assertion of their American identity reveals their great desire to be considered completely American and to leave their Italian roots in the past. But, of course, that was difficult for them, especially since both of them recalled an example of hatred that occurred in their youth. Edward said that near Hershey in Palmdale and Palmyra, some people were not only anti-Italian but anti-Catholic as well. He indi-

cated that a strong Ku Klux Klan organization existed in the area at one
time:

> They burned crosses in the field right next to our place where I was
> born. Where our church [St. Joan of Arc Roman Catholic Church] is
> now, that used to be a favorite place of theirs to burn crosses.[36]

Edward attended school and was involved in playing drums in the
drum and bugle corps. While in school, he started working in a barber-
shop shining shoes and cleaning. In school he attended the vocational
program learning industrial arts, electricity, the building trades, wood-
working, and sheet metal as well as business. Mr. Hershey wanted this
program in order to train future employees in mechanical and electrical
work. Edward enjoyed school, including the academic subjects as well.
His older brother Samuel had to quit high school to work for Hershey in
order to support the family because his father's illness prevented him
from working.

After high school he was already working for Hershey and therefore
did not go on to day junior college but attended at night. The group of
students with whom he attended went on to eventually become managers with the Hershey Chocolate enterprise. Edward started as a laborer
but wanted a better career. Mr. Zoll, who was in charge of hiring at the
time, told Edward that if he wanted a better job with Hershey, he would
have to quit his job as a laborer (working outside) and then apply for a
job in the factory itself. After Edward followed Mr. Zoll's directions and
quit his laborer's job, Mr. Zoll refused to hire him in the factory and told
him that he could hire him back only as a laborer. Mr. Zoll went back on
his word. Edward then searched for a job for three months during the
Depression and then wrote a letter to Mr. Murrie, the president of Hershey Chocolate at the time. He knew Mr. Murrie personally because he
had caddied for him. Finally, this effort succeeded and Edward started in
the factory as an electrical helper. Edward used his caddying experience
to make a connection and obtain a job in the Hershey Chocolate enterprise. Edward Tancredi overcame the fact that his last name ended in a
vowel.

Soon Edward was promoted to the position of journeyman and had
his own helper. Two years after Edward was hired, the sit-down strike
began at Hershey Chocolate on April 2, 1937. According to Edward, the
sit-down strike began because of incompetent management and low
wages—forty-two cents or forty-three cents per hour for men. Women's
wages were even lower. The farmers could not sell their milk to Hershey
Chocolate anymore so, according to Edward, they marched into the factory and threw the workers out and although he was not present at the
time, he was told that there was violence including "clubbing" to punish
the strikers. He also indicated that he was told that farmers had perpetrated this violence, but then he added a note of doubt: "but whoever it

was, I don't know."[37] This uncertainty reflects the suspicion that strike-breakers may have been hired to end the strike and were camouflaged as farmers. This suspicion was also aired by Lola Romanucci Ross who revealed some evidence of a plot that will be discussed in our analysis of her autobiographical text later in this study.

Edward also went further and implied that the Italian workers and others may have been subjected to abuse by managers. He stated that those "of Italian heritage, you have difficulty, one thing or another. Those days, the boss, the foreman, was lord and master. You heard that before."[38] The interviewer responds, "I've heard that" and Edward responds, "Okay. And being lord and master, they could do as they damn pleased. Some people were really abused. So that brought this whole thing on [the sit-down strike]."[39]

However, then Edward retreats somewhat from this strong statement: "The ones that need a union are the ones that get themselves in trouble."[40] He obviously hated violence and wanted everyone to get along better, but he did see value in the strike because he indicated that the union and management ultimately did cooperate and salaries and benefits improved greatly over the long term. Hershey Chocolate became a great place to work and a magnet for employment in Pennsylvania.

Despite his membership in the union, the company did not hold that against Edward, and he became a group leader and was considered so important that he received a draft deferment for his electrical work in manufacturing the "Army Bar" also known as the ration bar which tasted like chocolate but was more chewy and nutritious for the troops in World War II. In addition, Edward was promoted to Coordinator of Shop Trades, and then Supervisor of Mechanical Trades. Under his leadership, machinery was installed to negate the need for human handling of the chocolate product.

Edward seemed very positive in his assessment of the effect of World War II on the Hershey community and the company; he said that because of the unity inspired by the war effort, "we worked very close together. The community and the company. I don't think we had any problem during the war. . . . I think everything was very harmonious."[41] This statement coincides with Angelo Elmi's belief that the sacrifices of Italian Americans of Hershey for the war effort made an improvement in the relations among and between the Pennsylvania Dutch, other non-Italians and the Italian Americans in the Hershey area.

In his view of Milton S. Hershey, the great founder of the company, and the town of Hershey, Edward Tancredi showed much respect. Edward believed that after Mr. Hershey's death, the townspeople were at a loss and had to fend for themselves in caring for the infrastructure and the upkeep of high standards in maintaining the urban garden landscape that Mr. Hershey had developed. Also, he noted that after Mr. Hershey died, the feeling of security in the town diminished and the moral authority instilled by Mr. Hershey, who insisted on good behavior and a good work ethic among his employees, also weakened.

Edward also indicated that Mr. Hershey felt hurt and disappointment as a result of the 1937 strike because the people surrounding him in whom he placed faith and trust had not fully informed him about his employees' need to correct problems. They did not tell him the "full story" and he never expected his beloved employees to engage in a sit-down strike, according to Edward.[42]

Edward also discussed the 1953 strike when management lived in the plant day and night, and the company brought in wives and even children to keep the chocolate plant going. The reason for the strike was once again wages and a new problem, the increase in speed of production. Edward stated that there was fear of violence in the 1953 strike, and he felt fear while walking home alone. After the strike normalcy prevailed, a union shop was enforced, but Edward indicated that he did not believe in a union shop. Obviously, his management position in the company had changed his perspective from his previously more union-oriented point of view.

Increased unity in the town of Hershey resulted from the efforts the town and the company exerted to combat the destruction of Hurricane Agnes in the early seventies as well as the crisis of Three Mile Island in 1979. Three Mile Island was only five or six miles from Hershey. All ethnic groups came together to survive these crises.

Edward Tancredi's accomplishments are remarkable considering the difficulties his immigrant parents and his siblings and he himself experienced before 1920 — poverty and illness, and later, prejudice, that he overcame to gain meaningful employment. Edward prevailed and persevered and made great contributions to the Hershey Chocolate enterprise as well as to the community. His mother's desire that her children obtain an education motivated him to attend night school; like Angelo Elmi, he overcame the obstacles to become a manager at Hershey Chocolate, and he fully understood the need for better relations between management and labor as reflected in his sensitive discussion of the 1937 strike. He was a wise man.

Edward, like Angelo Elmi, experienced an internal conflict and could see the paradox facing him, which was dramatized in D'Antonio's *Hershey:*

> Edward Tancredi's name was on the Hershey Company's roster of strikers, which was sort of an enemy's list of strikers, with the annotation "active CIO." He was also an Italian-American Catholic who never forgot that crosses had been burned near his family's home and that some landlords in Hershey wouldn't rent to immigrants. But even after the strike, the riot, and a host of other insults, he like so many others in town would speak fondly of Mr. Hershey and credit him with what

was good and fair about the company and the place that bore his name.[43]

Both Edward Tancredi and Angelo Elmi resolved the duality of being both Italian and American by choosing to be as American as possible in the workplace and in public in order to survive and prosper in Hershey, Pennsylvania, the ultimate American town. What could be more American than the Hershey bar? They both prospered in the patriarchal social structure set in place by Mr. Hershey, a social pattern not so different from their origins in Italy. Angelo and Edward never forgot their roots.

ORAL HISTORY OF SAMUEL TANCREDI

Edward Tancredi's older brother, Samuel Tancredi, gave more details about the Tancredi family background and the early years in Hershey after his parents came to America. Samuel was born on April 16, 1914, two years before his brother Edward. His father, Antonio, and his mother, Louisa, had few opportunities in Italy, the same reason Angelo Elmi's parents left Tuscany. Samuel said that his father grew vegetables and sold them at a market in the city of Ascoli Piceno. He also sold wine which he made from his small vineyard. Antonio came to America by himself through Ellis Island in 1905, and Samuel's mother and three daughters came in 1907. Antonio attended school in Italy for eight years. Louisa never attended school and therefore as Edward said — she could not read. Antonio's first job in America was working for the Pennsylvania Railroad. He then worked in a Bedford, Pennsylvania steel mill. By that time the Tancredis had two sons and three daughters, but both sons died of pneumonia in 1913, and the oldest daughter, as Edward reported, died of influenza in 1918. Antonio's work in the steel mill was to pull coke out of furnaces, and Samuel describes this grueling experience:

> at night it might be raining or snowing and freezing on his back while he'd be baking on the front because of the burners.[44]

Ultimately, through a friend in Hershey, the Tancredis moved there where Antonio found a job in the Bradley quarries in 1909. Then Antonio became employed by Hershey Estates (another of Mr. Hershey's enterprises, which operated Hershey Park and other entities in Hershey). Samuel corroborated information provided by Edward that their sisters began work as children at age 11 and 12. He also notes his brother, Edward's birth in 1916. Unfortunately, Antonio was injured in work-related incidents, but because he did not receive workmen's compensation, his daughters and Samuel had to begin working. Samuel quit school at the age of 15 and started working for the Hershey Chocolate Company. Before that he worked picking up litter in Hershey Park. With the complicity and encouragement of his school principal, Samuel lied his age as being 16 so that he could start working at Hershey when he was only 15.

At that time, according to Samuel, conditions were primitive by today's standards:

> Telephone service was sparse. Trolley service was available on a straight line between towns. Travel in any other direction was mostly by walking. Farms had horses but townspeople did not. I remember only a handful of autos in town. Cultural activities, at least for the majority of us were very limited.[45]

Because of his father's infirmity, the family's finances were negatively affected, and Mrs. Murrie, the wife of the then president of the Chocolate Company, helped Samuel obtain a job. He started in the Mill Room in the factory and had no time for lunch; he worked twelve hours a day, six days a week for low pay. Workers could work seven days a week if they wanted to. Soon he was transferred to the office in August of 1929 at the mailing desk as an office boy. Mrs. Murrie encouraged Samuel to return to school at night. He then attended night school in Harrisburg and had to hitch a ride for the twelve-mile trip because he did not own an automobile. He had to complete several courses to earn his high school diploma so that he could attend the Wharton Extension School in Harrisburg. After that, he attended Hershey Junior College at night and graduated.

After one year as an office boy, Samuel was assigned to the Order and Billing Department where he handled customer service. Then he was transferred to the Sales Record Department and was working there when, in 1931, an IBM machine was installed. Other IBM machines had been installed even earlier—in 1926 or 27. According to Samuel, Hershey Chocolate Company was one of the first industrial concerns to use IBM. Prior to that only the government, namely the Census Bureau, used IBM machines. This marked the beginning of a stellar career for Samuel at Hershey.

Having attended night school for seventeen years while working full-time, Samuel had little or no social life. His only diversion appeared to be his involvement with music. His father Antonio wanted him to have a special skill which had been denied him because of the Tancredis' straitened circumstances in earlier years. Antonio arranged music lessons for Samuel, and he played the piccolo. Samuel found time in his hectic schedule to play in the old Hershey band and the Palmyra Iroquois Band. He was invited to play in the Harrisburg Symphony Orchestra but could not because he was always working, studying, and attending night school. He found school exciting, and he was admirably prepared for his financial focus at work. He became Supervisor of the Tabulating Department. There he began applying computers to solve problems and enhance the efficiency of the company.

During the Depression Samuel took note of the duality in Mr. Hershey's style of leadership. He could fire people on the spot if they were not working up to his standards; on the other hand, he created a lot of work and kept people employed during the Depression not only in the chocolate factory but also in major construction projects in the town of Hershey. Growing up in Hershey as children, one always heard that there was no Depression in Hershey, Pennsylvania. Mr. Hershey was creating lucrative real estate and keeping people employed while making profits for himself and financing his philanthropic project—the development of the Hershey Industrial School, now known as the Milton S. Hershey School for children who had no parents or had only one parent.

By 1947, after Mr. Hershey's death and the end of World War II, Samuel was promoted to a higher level management position. This was quite an accomplishment for a thirty-four year old Italian American who could not speak much English as a child until he began attending school. He could not even understand his teacher; as a result, his principal assumed that Samuel had misbehaved and was disobedient. Samuel said, "He gave me a hell of a good whaling." [46] Instead of seeing this incident as discriminatory and abusive, as many of us would today, Samuel justified the punishment because he believed the teacher might have thought he was misbehaving on purpose.

Samuel enjoyed school and was nostalgic about Hershey Junior College and wished it had not closed in the mid-sixties. The dean at Hershey Junior College then became the dean at Franklin and Marshall College where Samuel's son Bob was to become a student. Samuel spoke to the dean about his son Bob's chances to become a doctor since he had read that: "young people of Italian and Jewish origin were being kept on a very severe quota insofar as entrance into medical school was concerned." [47]

Samuel's concerns came to naught because Bob did enter Franklin and Marshall College and graduated from the University of Pennsylvania, School of Medicine on scholarship in 1958. He became a cardiologist and at the time of this oral history interview, Bob Tancredi had become a member of the Mayo Board of Governors and the Board of Trustees. Samuel's second son, Larry, had to attend Hershey Junior College because Samuel was on a tight budget at that time, but he also completed his undergraduate degree at Franklin and Marshall College and earned his M.D. at the University of Pennsylvania School of Medicine and went on to Yale law School. Larry is both a psychiatrist and a lawyer and has had a stellar career, having published many articles and books.

Samuel then reminisces in general about the obstacles in his path upward to a successful career and life, but singles out prejudice: "I've had some pretty bad things happen to me. I've encountered prejudice along the way, my family has too, and those things are never going to stop." [48] But he justifies this prejudice as normal for "new people" and not aimed at immigrants and their children as individuals, "just whatever crazy things there are in people" that make these things happen."[49]

In his memories, his courtship of his wife Alvesta, known as Vae, stood out as a very happy time. They married in 1936. Vae, like Samuel, had also quit school to work in the chocolate factory. She worked there for seven years. Samuel stated that the custom among Italians at that time was that boys needed an education but girls did not. Samuel implied that this was unfortunate because Vae was an excellent student. Ironically, after they were married, Samuel wanted Vae to quit her job because he believed that women who worked in the factory burned out in their forties, and he did not want that for her. He had seen that too often. Therefore, he went to Mr. Zoll and arranged for Vae to quit her job: "My wife didn't like it, but she didn't leave me. So you know, it was nice to have a couple of kids and go on from there."[50]

Obviously, Samuel wanted so much more for his wife and children than his parents could have done for him.

Like his father, Samuel felt it was important for his sons to develop a special skill in music. His son Bob is a fine pianist who played at a concert with the Rochester Symphony and also played when he was younger in Hershey at the Lutheran Church.

Samuel then recounted an amusing incident when he himself was only in fourth grade and played in a group at a Protestant Church. The Catholic priest at the time became upset and went to Samuel's parents to discourage this. But his father Antonio, who spoke only broken English, answered the priest: "You know, I just can't understand how it can be bad for anybody to help somebody worship God. How can that be bad?"[51] The wisdom of an Italian immigrant with only eight years of education in Italy is illustrated in that simple but pointed statement.

When asked about the 1937 strike, Samuel expanded on his brother Edward and Angelo Elmi's statements on that subject. Samuel explained, like Edward, that the pay at Hershey Chocolate in 1937 was notoriously low. He realized this later because he then became responsible for the payroll and knew the pay given by other companies in other parts of Pennsylvania. Also, working conditions were difficult at Hershey Chocolate; according to Samuel, even the "lowliest foreman could fire you."[52] Samuel also believed that an article read by many people in Hershey called attention to the fact that the Hershey Industrial School, Mr. Hershey's philanthropic creation for orphan boys at the time, was spending $3000 per year to maintain a child but the typical employee made much less and had to support a family. Samuel believed that the article represented very poor public relations on the part of Hershey Chocolate. His reaction also illustrates his loyalty to the company as well as his perspicacity about the importance of image in business. However, the objective observer can readily comprehend the anger of the workers in noting the disparity between Mr. Hershey's generous charity and the miserly pay they were receiving to support their families.

Samuel also noted that no Italian was in the union leadership, "but they got the blame for bringing it [the strike] on."[53] Because he was part of management, Samuel worked throughout the strike and reported a vicious act of violence perpetrated by either the strikers or the strike-breakers. He did not know which. A young man named Mr. Sponaugle was stabbed in the stomach with an ice pick. Fortunately, Mr. Sponaugle recovered and became a good friend of both Samuel Tancredi and Angelo Elmi.

Samuel then noted the hatred for the Italian workers on whom it was easy to lay the blame for the strike even though they were not in the union leadership:

> There was a lot of hate material published in those days, too, Dick. I remember pamphlets titled "Swat that fly," and when you read the text of the articles, they were talking about the Italian people. We weren't all up there on the wrong side, you know, but that's the way it was being presented. And there was a booklet, *Civil War in Hershey Town*. Maybe you've seen it.[54]

The interviewer denies seeing this pamphlet, but Sam retorts, "That, too talks about it. Those are the sad things that happened."[55] Samuel obviously considered the strikers to be on the wrong side of the issue while, on the other hand, he knew that they were egregiously underpaid. After all, Samuel was loyal to management. However, he resented the vilification of the Italians of Hershey. One can readily perceive some role conflict in Samuel's reaction, not so different from his brother Edward or his colleague, Angelo Elmi.

Samuel, like Edward, received a draft deferment during World War II. The reason for the deferment was that in Samuel's case, he already had two children.

Samuel praised the contributions of Mr. Hershey in creating jobs for thousands of people for generations. He then elaborated on his position in the company as a Director of Information Systems and giving financial information to management. He discussed the improvement in developing sales forecasting for planning production, inventory, supplies, raw materials procurement, facilities and personnel required. He explained the relationship of sales forecasting to cost accounting, budgeting, manufacturing, sales, marketing, demand for the product, raw materials needed, storage, and inventory.[56]

Samuel was also involved in planning the California factory and stressed the need for cooperation and coordination of efforts. In 1960 he was appointed Assistant Treasurer of the company and his tasks were expanded to include "salary, factory and milk payrolls, sales records, order approval, credit administration, and central office services department."[57] Samuel had little to do with the 1953 strike because he was too busy working, but he did say that although that strike was ugly, there was no violence. Samuel also stated that the 1937 strike need not have happened. He indicated that rampant union activity around the United States had created an environment for a strike in Hershey to obtain wage increases, especially since newspapers were publishing increases in pay as a result of union activity across the country. He then reiterated his previous statement that pay in the Hershey factory was well below 50 cents an hour and that announced pay increases of 5 percent were too small:

> Thus making the situation more pungent the company announced a hefty increase to take effect on either March 1 or April 1. This time I recall vividly salaries, including my own, were increased by 20 percent. The plant hourly rates were materially increased, also, but I don't recall how much. This enabled the union leadership to say, "You see? We've got these guys scared. They haven't been treating you right and they've been pouring it on you." They had the workers thinking that they were going to open up the company treasury now and give it to them. Then the 1937 strike happened.[58]

After making this statement, which could be interpreted as having some sympathy for the strikers while maintaining a superficial pro-management stance, Samuel became concerned that this oral history would become public knowledge. It seemed as though he was trying to preserve the confidentiality of his complex view of the 1937 strike: "Now, I worry about it when you say you're going to show this out in public."[59] The interviewer tried to allay Samuel's anxiety: "Most of the people who use this thing will be historians, and they understand. They studied American history"[60]

Samuel responded: "No, for some jobs it was fine."[61] It seemed as if the interviewer was comforting Sam about the low pay the Hershey Chocolate workers had been receiving before the 1937 strike. The interviewer noted that "Anybody will have to read this and will have to be serious about what they are doing so that's what we carry into that."[62] The interviewer seemed to encourage Samuel to trust the integrity and objectivity of historians in studying the oral histories in the Hershey Archive and writing about them.

In the remainder of his oral history, Samuel analyzes the various top administrators of the company in a serious and productive manner. His intelligence, wisdom, and acumen in business and in life—his loyalty and honesty—make one wonder whether in a better, fairer world, he could have risen even higher in the company, even to become president. It is obvious he would have made a superb corporate leader.

Samuel's oral history shows that he had become the ultimate company man and that although he could understand the plight of workers who made low pay during the Depression, he wished mightily that the 1937 strike had never occurred; meanwhile he also resented the way Italians were made to look scurrilous and negative when they were only trying to follow union efforts to gain better pay. Samuel had suffered as a young boy in seeing his father incapacitated and experiencing the deaths of his siblings. He made enormous sacrifices to help support his family and rose to a position of upper management at Hershey Chocolate even though he started as only an office boy. He made certain that he obtained an education by attending night school for seventeen years, and he motivated his sons to become outstanding professional men with an Ivy League education. Samuel could not have done all of this without the help and support of his wife Alvesta. He overcame the obstacle of prejudice through diligence and self-sacrifice. Like Angelo Elmi and his brother Edward, Samuel thrived in the patriarchal environment of Hershey, Pennsylvania. Samuel was more circumspect in revealing his internal conflict—being Italian in the ultimate American corporate world at that time in history. His internal conflict, then, was buried deeper than the dilemmas faced by Angelo Elmi and Edward Tancredi, yet he was an excellent Italian son to his Italian parents as well as a model parent to his Italian American sons. His family values show that he never lost sight of his Italian background.

INTERVIEWS OF ALVESTA "VAE" TANCREDI

Although there is no oral history of Alvesta "Vae" Tancredi, her life in Hershey was described in an article spanning two newsletters of *Reflections: The Newsletter of the Hershey Derry Township Historical Society:* The January/February/March edition as well as the April/May/June 2015 edition. Alvesta Tancredi along with her neighbor, Stephanie Sopcak, were interviewed about Alvesta's life in Hershey as she turned 100. As of this writing she is 105. The author of the article in *Reflections,* "100 Years of Memories: A personal History of Vae Tancredi, "is Emily Grace Murray who came to Hershey at the age of six. Murray states that Vae at the age of 100 "stands as witness to the formation, growth, and evolution of a small central Pennsylvania town into an American triumph.[63] Vae stated that despite the opportunity for work in the stone quarries, her father, Iroldo Pera, "wouldn't go in the stone quarries. . . . He waited for the chocolate factory and then worked for Hershey Foods" [Hershey Chocolate had once been known as Hershey Foods; now it is the Hershey Company].[64] Alvesta's father was a very close friend of Angelo Elmi's father, Francesco Elmi. The Elmis, the Peras, and the Tancredis (Samuel's family) all lived on West Granada Avenue, within a block of each other in a new Little Italy in Hershey. Alvesta's mother was Latina Pera who was also from Italy. Vae had two siblings, Nancy Pera who was born in 1912 and

Albert Pera who was born in 1916. He and Angelo Elmi became good friends. Vae was born on June 26, 1914. Because her mother was ill after Vae was born, she could not nurse her. Therefore, Samuel Tancredi's mother Louisa who was still nursing him (he was born on April 16, 1914) agreed to nurse both Vae and Sam. Vae recalls being told that a comment was made when Louisa was nursing both babies: "Wouldn't it be funny if they were to grow up and get married one day?"[65] Vae then recalled seeing Mr. Hershey in his chauffeur-driven car. She remembered living and playing near Hershey Park, riding the roller coaster (the Wildcat), and the carousel, boating on the lake, and attending shows at the bandstand where Frank Sinatra appeared. She also recalled the Starlight Ballroom where Guy Lombardo appeared, and where she danced as a young girl. Vae also reminisced about the beautiful swimming pool and the fountain with colored lights. Vae reminded readers about the fact that that swimming pool and the marvelous Starlight Ballroom no longer exist, having given way to the enlargement of Hershey Park and the edifice known as Chocolate World, a giant retail space and ride through an artificial demonstration of the manufacturing of chocolate since the Hershey Chocolate factory has been remodeled and tours of the actual chocolate factory ended years ago.

Vae also reminisced about life in the new Little Italy on West Granada Avenue. She described the lush gardens, the source of fresh vegetables, and the many trees that provided fresh fruit—apples, cherries, peaches, and apricots, for example on the Elmi property half a block from Alvesta's house. She also spoke of the produce, milk, meat, and eggs that were delivered to the neighborhood by itinerant farmers and sales people as well as the grocery store in the neighborhood where on payday families would pay their bills. Alvesta also described the social life encouraged by interaction among Italian immigrants and their children on their closely aligned front porches. The life Vae describes on West Granada Avenue seemed idyllic in the old days and this writer can substantiate her impressions since he lived there for seventeen years as a child and teenager. Vae's portrait of Hershey in her youth and young adulthood reflects the beauty and organization of Mr. Hershey's planned community as depicted by McMahon's portrait of Hershey in *Built on Chocolate: The Story of the Hershey Chocolate Company.*[66]

When she was asked about ethnic tensions in Hershey, Vae painted a different picture, but did not elaborate: "The Italians had it rough in this town. . . . Everybody knows it. . . . It was terrible in the beginning."[67] And her neighbor added to this statement: "What happened is what you have happen in most places when you have new people coming. There's always somebody who's low man on the totem pole. And the Italians really did work hard here. They brought themselves up and did really well"[68] Vae's neighbor Stephanie also stated that Mr. Hershey was not part of the discriminatory treatment of Italians: "though tensions were really high between the Pennsylvanian Dutch and the Italians, Mr. Hershey, the central figure of the town, remained remarkably open-minded and kind" adding: "He would stop and ask how the Italians grew their crops. He'd ask my grandfather about his fig trees. He'd go down the alley and look at the gardens and he wanted to learn from them. He was a very accepting person. Anywhere you go you have people who think with smaller minds but he seemed to embrace [differences] pretty well." [69]

Vae then described her courtship and marriage to Samuel Tancredi, corroborating Samuel's statement in his oral history and his insistence on her quitting her job to become the mother of her sons Bob and Larry. Also in the Murray interview, Vae referred to her husband's relentless pursuit of education in spite of his full-time job at Hershey Chocolate. He created "an arsenal of degrees," according to Vae. [70] Obviously, Vae was very proud of Samuel's educational accomplishments, given the difficult odds he faced as the son of immigrants.

As time passed, it became clear that many non-Italians realized that Italian Americans were as qualified for progress in America as any other ethnic group who had preceded them in this country. Vae also indicated that her sons also were treated well in the Hershey public schools. This was not always the case, unfortunately. But later in this study, Lola Romanucci-Ross makes a statement that partially explains why the Tancredis and she herself were treated well in the Hershey schools—for the most part.

In agreement with Angelo Elmi, Edward Tancredi, and her husband Samuel, Vae stated that after Pearl Harbor, great changes took place in Hershey: women replaced men in the factory because many men were drafted. She also described the reaction of the town when Mr. Hershey died in 1945: "When he died, we went to the viewing in the Hotel . . . everybody felt sad" [71]

Vae's description of West Granada Avenue Italian American life in Hershey contributed to the history of Italian Americans in the broader sense, for they have transformed many urban and suburban neighborhoods across the country with their gardens and well-kept homes no matter whether they were rich or poor. Vae was in a sense the most well-known and one of the most beautiful women in Hershey. In spite of the fact that her parents had come from another country and experienced difficulty at first in Hershey, Vae was able to live a fulfilling life in her marriage and in her role in the community and, most important, in her role as a mother who motivated both her sons to obtain an Ivy League education and establish themselves in highly successful professional careers. Vae represents a 105 years of a transformative life as an Italian American. She is a role model for others in the Italian American community and other immigrant communities to follow.

LOLA ROMANUCCI-ROSS: BORN IN
HERSHEY, LATER, A CITIZEN OF THE WORLD

Like Vae, Lola Romanucci Ross did not record an oral history in the Hershey Archive. However, as a professor and anthropologist, Lola wrote a book entitled *To Love a Stranger: The Making of an Anthropologist.* This autobiographical text describes her development into becoming a renowned professor and scholar, a great accomplishment for the daughter of Italian immigrants in Hershey, Pennsylvania. Lola Romanucci-Ross is a cousin of the Tancredis. Her parents came from an area near the city of Ascoli Piceno in Le Marche, but she traced her maternal ancestry, the Celani family (her maternal grandmother), to Abruzzi where they may have owned a castle known as Celano.[72] Her maternal grandmother was from Malva, a mountain village close to Ascoli Piceno. Lola indicated that the Romanucci name is a diminutive of Romani; however, the family most probably originated in the Veneto in the 1500s and then moved south.[73] Lola Romanucci Ross eventually broke away from the patriarchal society she was born into in Hershey, Pennsylvania, unlike Angelo Elmi, the Tancredi brothers, Alvesta Tancredi and many other Italian Americans in Mr. Hershey's Chocolate Kingdom. However, she has not forgotten her roots. Lola revealed in her autobiography *To Love a Stranger: The Making of an Anthropologist* and that she traveled from alienation in her childhood in Hershey to a sense of being a part of the world community as an adult anthropologist.[74]

Lola's father, Ignazio Romanucci had a great influence on her. Her maternal grandmother, Giulia Celani, admired Ignazio as remarkably intelligent.[75] Most of her mother Peppina's friends in Hershey considered Lola to be "possessed by an evil being" because she could speak at the age of nine months and because Ignazio never attended mass and would not allow Peppina to attend either, nor did he permit any religious Catholic images or icons to be displayed; instead, he displayed a portrait of Giacomomo Matteotti, a well-known anti-fascist martyr.[76] Her mother's friends also considered Lola to be a "devil child . . . badly in need of Baptism in the Catholic Church;" therefore her mother had Lola baptized secretly.[77] Lola was even subjected to the ritual of removing malocchio, the evil eye.[78] However Lola stated that she lied to her Zia Gigetta Aunt Luigia, who performed the ritual, about becoming Catholic because she could not lie to her father. Thus, even as a child Lola felt the power of liberation from institutional religious confinement and patriarchal domination—in this case, freedom from Catholic rules including such rituals as sacramental baptism. Truly, Ignazio Romanucci and his daughter questioned and flouted patriarchal societal structures that threatened to confine them intellectually and morally.

In the Hershey schools, Lola excelled despite the fact the teachers had problems understanding the Italian immigrant culture.[79] In addition, the various Protestant congregations and Republicans dominating Hershey at the time strongly disliked the Catholic religion.[80]

Lola herself felt lonely in the Hershey public schools because her playmates from Swatara, who were the children of Italian immigrants like herself, all attended St. Joan of Arc Catholic School, and she noted that at lunchtime she was the only child whose lunch consisted of a large sandwich in Italian bread wrapped in waxed paper and covered over by pages from an Italian newspaper while the non-Italian children simply ate sliced bread sandwiches.[81]. If she was tormented on the playground, Lola's revenge was to earn high grades in order to have her name on the honor roll.[82]

Lola observed that Italian immigrant parents imposed "gendered spaces" on children when they reached the age of puberty. Unwanted pregnancies were to be avoided and the honor of the family name was to be upheld.[83]

Lola also observed that women's work at that time was physical including laundry, making pasta by hand, never eating packaged food, growing vegetables in the garden, sewing dresses and underwear, repairing outworn clothing, making soap and taking care of their children.[84] Lola also discussed the social lives of the Italian immigrant women quite accurately: their ritualistic visits where coffee and biscotti were served, and gossip about the lives of others was the focus.[85] Lola's rendition of the Italian women's social gatherings was exactly as this writer remembers them as a child when listening to their gossip and grabbing a biscotto. It was an easy way for anyone to learn Italian. She further indicated that the women were more interesting to observe than the men because men were always working, but she did focus on the male culture of winemaking as well as their interest in world events.[86]

Lola indicated that her father Ignazio was a human being of worthy principles and knowledge.[87] Ignazio created an intellectual milieu for his daughter. He himself spent his time away from work reading rather than socializing like other Italian immigrants in Hershey, and he had a library consisting of impressive books including a number of the classic works.[88]

Lola recounted the experience Ignazio had in World War I, which led to a major reason for his departure from Italy. Ignazio was forced by the circumstances of war to kill a young Austrian soldier who was Catholic like him.[89] Disillusioned by this pivotal experience, Ignazio then stopped attending mass and became involved in anti-fascist, anti-militaristic politics in Italy. He then left Italy to go to the United States, specifically Hershey, Pennsylvania.[90]

Lola then describes the negative effects of immigration, for example, the stress experienced by Italian women who could not adjust to life in Hershey; and Italian immigrants becoming victims of predatory Mafia style organized crime.[91] This terrible scourge may have led to an infamous murder in Hershey's Little Italy, which Lola describes as vicious and bloody.[92] Lola then notes the reaction of the Hershey Italian community to this event:

> They were stunned now fearing, 'the worst' which meant they would *all* be accused of harboring a lawless and violent small community of immigrants, and perhaps they themselves might be considered 'of the same stripe,' not an unrealistic scenario.[93]

The Italian community in Hershey never spoke of these matters again. The reaction of the Italian community—to remain silent for fear of being stereotyped as a center of organized crime—reflects their concern about potential discrimination.[94]

Lola made a telling comment about the Hershey Italian immigrant community's perspective on the African Americans who worked in Hershey. She indicated that the Italian immigrants noted the easier jobs African Americans had than they did and there was no resentment from the Italian immigrants. Moreover, according to Lola, the Italian immigrants wanted African Americans to be treated well.[95] However, she continues:

> In contrast, what Italians had to do to make a living was to work long hours in unpleasant surroundings and suffer the indignities of being referred to as "wops" or "dagos."[96]

Amusingly, then Lola refers to the Italian ability to "laugh off" such derision.[97] They had such in-jokes as perceiving the Pennsylvania Dutch as "slow," for example, in their schoolwork.[98] This was obviously a way of defending themselves from prejudice with private contempt for their target.

Lola indicated that her family did not experience such treatment from the non-Italian community because of her father's Calvinistic character, and the fact that even though they were Italian, they were not Catholic, which she referred to as "the most disliked religion in Hershey" at the time of her childhood and adolescence.[99] Often Italians and Italian Americans are instantly perceived as Catholic, but that is not always the case and can become another example of stereotyping.

To dramatize this dislike of Catholicism in the early days of the Italian community in Hershey, Lola refers to the Ku Klux Klan's attacks on the Catholic Church in Hershey:

> There were two attempts by the Ku Klux Klan to set fire to the St. Joan of Arc Church. In the second and last attempt, they were greeted by shots in the night (courtesy of several . . . protectors of the Faith). The Klan members fled immediately, never to return.[100]

Ironically, today, St. Joan of Arc Church is one of the most dynamic as well as the largest congregation In Hershey.

Lola also discusses the unionization of the workers in the Hershey Chocolate factory, the negative reaction of the company to unions, and the 1937 strike. Lola, like Samuel Tancredi, also describes an article in *Mill and Factory,* entitled "Civil War in Hershey Town" in which the Hershey Italian community was falsely described as Communist, where Italians sang Communist songs and believed in a revolution against America.[101] In this context she describes her father as having studied both Communism and Fascism. Lola's father considered Communism not any better than the Fascism of Mussolini and maybe Communism was worse.[102] This article, according to Lola, described Mr. Hershey as a "family man" who built houses for the workers, and it refers to the Pennsylvania Dutch and Dunkards as simple good people farmers, who had to come into Hershey to "break up the strike, so that the town might be liberated from this union pestilence."[103] However, Lola asserts the fact that the workers had mortgages from the Hershey Bank to pay for their houses. And another possible truth was that the simple farmers who came to town to break up the strike were possibly camouflaged paid strikebreakers.[104]

Indeed, Lola, who attended school with the children of non-Italian children had learned from them of the following scheme to break the strike. Hired professional strike-breakers from the Pittsburgh area ("the very best") had been outfitted as farmers, with appropriate attire; some had pitchforks in hand as well. These impostors who were to save the plant from the supposedly subversive Bolsheviks among the factory workers.[105] Lola observed the strike from her class, which was the only college preparatory group in the high school. She states: "I was one of two Italian-Americans in that class. Their syllogistic reasoning of the others was this: *wops* do not attend college; we both planned to do that, therefore we were not *wops*."[106] Learning of this plan to break the strike, Lola worried about her father Ignazio who had joined the strikers. The strike-breakers singled out the Italian workers who did not raise their arms in surrender as they left the plant and therefore "were beaten."[107] Fortunately, Ignazio was not harmed possibly because he did not fit the popular American stereotype of an Italian man, supposedly darker and more hirsute than the typical American.

However, he was punished in an even more iniquitous manner as time passed. Since he was not an American citizen, he was dismissed from the Hershey Chocolate plant and he had to go to court to face the accusation—"first, because the company had been told he was a Communist" and a second time after war had been declared against the Axis powers including Italy, "some of the informers stated that he was a Fascist."[108] Both cases, which came before the same judge, were dismissed. Ignazio made this statement before the judge:

> As for my beliefs, when I came to this country I escaped tyranny and reveled in the writings of Thomas Jefferson and Tom Paine. These are my Americans and their beliefs are mine, for mine had always been

theirs. Perhaps I believed these Americans too much for the reality I am experiencing now. [109]

After he dismissed the case, the judge responded: "This country would be blessed to have every immigrant who comes to these shores be like you." [110] The informers who had attempted to destroy the reputation of Lola's father must have been chastened to learn of their failure. Ignazio was too honest and too intelligent to be defeated by such prevaricators.

By the time these court cases had occurred, Lola had already gone away to college.

Indeed, Ignazio had prepared her for college away from Hershey to a place where a person would not be judged for being an Italian American. [111]

Ignazio Romanucci thus was far more advanced in his thinking than most of the other Italian immigrants of Hershey. At the time even though many of them valued education for their boys, they certainly did not think it was necessary for girls to be educated beyond high school, for they generally expected them to become secretaries and encouraged them to take the commercial track in grades 9 through 12. Meanwhile Lola went away to college at the University of Ohio in Athens, Ohio, a decision that most Italian immigrants, including this writer's grandparents, in the same generation as Ignazio, considered to be unthinkable. The immigrant generation in the 1930s expected their daughters to work after high school (if they had not already dropped out and were working in the chocolate factory), bring home their paychecks to their parents to help support the family, and then marry a man from the same town or region of Italy where their parents originated, have children and lead a domestic life. Breaking with that tradition with the encouragement and approval of her unconventional father and her understanding mother, Lola was off on many adventures and accomplished much as a professional, highly educated woman. Lola was a great role model for young Italian American women who wanted to go to college.

Lola graduated from college with a major in International Studies and Economic Theory, and started working for a U.S. Naval Depot, became a librarian at a U.S. Army Post, and then a union organizer for the Garment Workers Union (ILGWU) in the Carolinas and Tennessee where she temporarily changed her name to Romand because union headquarters ordered her to change her name. The union organizer did not want the people from these southern states to think that Italians and Jews were being sent to unionize their workshops. [112]

Eventually, she quit her union job and returned to Hershey, married, and moved to the Midwest where she led the life of a housewife for a time. However, she also earned a Master's degree from the University of Minnesota and eventually a Ph.D. in Anthropology from Indiana University; she also studied at the University of Chicago. [113] Lola needed intellectual stimulus; she had the opportunity to meet Erich Fromm and Margaret Mead, the famous anthropologist. Lola did anthropological fieldwork in Mexico, studied at the Sorbonne in Paris, at the Ecole Practique des Hautes Etudes, College de France. Lola also attended post-doctoral lectures in Paris given by the famous Professor Claude Levi Strauss. She performed so well in his class that he praised her.[114]

While she was in Paris, Lola became pregnant with her second child and intended to return to Hershey. Her anthropological reasoning was remarkable:

> I am, culturally, an Italian mother, and an Italian mother must have a Son. I asked the Madonna for this. . . . All things considered, in times like these, I needed to be with Ignazio and Peppina, to eat her meals, gossip with her, and to once again hear my father's impeccable Italian and his logical thinking.[115]

Lola thus longed to return to her Italian parents in Hershey for this important event in her life. In spite of her departure from the culturally limited Central Pennsylvania town she was born in and where she felt alienated not only from the community at large but also from many other Italian Americans in Hershey, she needed her home base and was honest about it.

Three months after Adan Anthony was born Lola took him to New Guinea in the Pacific. Before they left the States, Lola wrote that Margaret Mead prepared medicine for them as well as a medical manual to save lives at their Pacific destination where Lola was to do fieldwork in Melanesia.[116] Her professional life thus became a great success.

Lola was fluent in Spanish, Italian and French. She lectured in anthropology at the University of Hawaii and San Fernando University. From 1969 until retiring in 2007, Lola taught at the University of California of San Diego where she was promoted to Professor of Anthropology and Medical Anthropology in the Department of Family and Preventive Medicine, and Associated Faculty in the Department of Anthropology. She introduced the first course in Human Sexuality. Lola also lectured at the University of California of San Diego School of Medicine on medical anthropology and on the role of social and behavioral sciences in medicine. Lola has also authored 77 books and articles according to the Afterword, About the Author: Lola Romanucci-Ross, in *To Love the Stranger: The Making of an Anthropologist.*[117]

Thus Lola has fulfilled her father's dream of obtaining as much education as she desired. Lola broke free from the patriarchal social town and corporate world of Hershey. She was unusual for her generation of Italian American women. Unlike Alvesta Tancredi and others, through the enlightened parenting of Ignazio and her mother Peppina, Lola was encouraged and given the opportunity to obtain a higher education and go on to graduate school. She left Hershey and lived as a citizen of the world

and therefore surpassed Angelo Elmi and the Tancredi brothers in education. She made a great impact on many students and scholars as a role
model for women in the professions today. Before her time, she was a
liberated woman.

Also, as a result of her education and life away from Hershey, Lola
saw Hershey and the Chocolate Kingdom more objectively than the other
subjects of this study. Her book *To Love a Stranger: The Making of an
Anthropologist* gives a more detailed view of the social life of Italian immigrants and their children in Hershey than the Elmi and Tancredi brothers' oral histories. Indeed, however, it has to be said that her excellent
education in the Hershey public schools as well as the intellectual atmosphere fostered by her father with the cooperation of her mother laid the
foundation for her great leap forward in the world of American higher
education and the study of anthropology world-wide. But Lola Romanucci-Ross never forgot her origins in the Italian community of Hershey,
Pennsylvania. Angelo Elmi, the Tancredi brothers, and Alvesta Tancredi
deserve credit for their perseverance and accomplishments despite struggling against poverty and prejudice in the early days. Each of the individuals in this study, in his or her own way, contributed to the success and
renown of "the sweetest place on earth," Hershey, Pennsylvania.

NOTES

1. See Michael D'Antonio, *Hershey: Milton S. Hershey's Extraordinary Life of Wealth,
Empire, and Utopian Dreams,* Long Beach, NY, Simon and Schuster, 2006 and Natalie
Mykta Dekle, *Building a New Life: The Italian Community in Hershey.* Hershey, PA:
Italian Lodge, 1990.
2. See Paul A.W. Wallace and Katherine B. Shippen, *Milton S. Hershey.* From *Biog-
raphy of Milton S. Hershey.* n.p. New York: Random House, 1959, 34.
3. See Michael D'Antonio, *Hershey: Milton S. Hershey's Extraordinary Life of Wealth,
Empire, and Utopian Dreams,* Long Beach, NY, Simon and Schuster, 2006 and Natalie
Mykta Dekle, *Building a New Life: The Italian Community in Hershey.* Hershey, PA:
Italian Lodge, 1990.
4. See Natalie Mykta Dekle, *Building a New Life: The Italian Community in Hershey.*
Hershey, PA: Italian Lodge, 1990.
5. See Paul A.W. Wallace and Katherine B. Shippen, *Milton S. Hershey.* From *Biog-
raphy of Milton S. Hershey.* n.p. New York: Random House, 1959.
6. See Michael D'Antonio, *Hershey: Milton S. Hershey's Extraordinary Life of Wealth,
Empire, and Utopian Dreams,* Long Beach, NY, Simon and Schuster, 2006, 104.
7. Ibid., 122.
8. See Michael D'Antonio, *Hershey: Milton S. Hershey's Extraordinary Life of Wealth,
Empire, and Utopian Dreams,* Long Beach, NY, Simon and Schuster, 2006 and Natalie
Mykta Dekle, *Building a New Life: The Italian Community in Hershey.* Hershey, PA:
Italian Lodge, 1990.
9. See Angelo Elmi, Oral History Interview with Angelo Elmi by Matthew Loser,
Hershey Community Archives Oral History Collection, Hershey, PA, 1998 (1/27/1998,
980H101, 2).
10. See Giuseppe Formiconi and Mauro Dreassi, *Pitigliano: Guida Turistica,* Pitiglia-
no, Grosseto, Italia, Pitigliano Consilio di Amministrazione della Cassa Rurale ed
Artgigiano di Pitigliano A.T., 1985, 6. This is partially based on the 1787 notes of the

Grand Duke of Tuscany of the Hapsburg-Lorraine dynasty, Pietro Leopoldo, when Tuscany was under Austrian control. (Gina Macchiarulo Elmi trans.)

11. Ibid.

12. See Eamon Duffy, *Saints and Sinners: A History of Popes,* New Haven: Yale University Press, 1987, 169.

13. See Formiconi and Dreassi, *Pitigliano: Guida Turistica,* 16, and Giuseppe Celata, *The Jews of Pitigliano: Four Centuries of a Diverse Community,* Pitigliano, Grosseto, Italy, N.P. Printed by A.T.L A., 20015–138.

14. Ibid.

15. See Lola Romanucci-Ross. *To Love the Stranger: The Making of an Anthropologist,* Charleston, Crate Space Independent Publishing Platform, 2012, 59.

16. Ibid.

17. The author Francis N. Elmi recently visited Pitigliano and personally observed the changes.

18. See D'Antonio, *Hershey: Milton Hershey's Extraordinary Life of Wealth, Empire and Utopian Dreams, 2006,* 244.

19. See Ascoli Piceno, *The New Encyclopedia Britannica Micropaedia,* edited by the faculties of the University of Chicago, 15th edition, vol. 1, The University of Chicago, 1977 and Lola Romanucci Ross, *One Hundred Towers: An Italian Odyssey of Cultural Survival,* New York, Bergin and Garvey, 191, 33–46.

20. See Angelo Elmi, Oral History Interview with Angelo Elmi by Matthew Loser, Hershey Community Archives Oral History Collection, Hershey, PA, 1998 (1/27/1998, 980H101, 2).

21. Ibid.

22. See Natalie Mykta Dekle, *Building a New Life: The Italian Community in Hershey.* Hershey, PA: Italian Lodge, 1990.

23. Angelo Elmi, Oral History Interview, (1/27/1998), 25.

24. See Angelo Elmi, Oral History Interview with Angelo Elmi by Matthew Loser, Hershey Community Archives Oral History Collection, Hershey, PA, 1998 (1/27/1998, 980H101, 2).

25. Ibid., 30.

26. Ibid.

27. See Angelo Elmi, Oral History Interview with Angelo Elmi by Matthew Loser, Hershey Community Archives Oral History Collection, Hershey, PA, 1998 (1/27/1998, 980H101, 2).

28. Ibid.

29. Angelo Elmi, Oral History Interview, (1/27/1998), 7.

30. Ibid.

31. Ibid., 8.

32. See Edward C. Tancredi, Oral History Interview with Edward C. Tancredi by Matthew Loser, Hershey Community Archives Oral History Collection, Hershey, PA (9/8/1991, 910H27,3).

33. Ibid., 7.

34. Ibid.

35. Ibid.

36. Ibid., 8.

37. Ibid., 21.

38. Ibid., 22.

39. Ibid.

40. Ibid.

41. Ibid., 34.

42. Ibid., 42–43.

43. See D'Antonio, *Milton Hershey's Extraordinary Life of Wealth, Empire, and Utopian Dreams,* 2006, 221.

44. See Samuel N. Tancredi, Oral History Interview by Richard Williams, Hershey Community Archives Oral History Collection, Hershey, PA (7/30/1990, 900H18, 2).

45. Ibid., 3.
46. Ibid., 13.
47. Ibid., 15.
48. Ibid.
49. Ibid.
50. Ibid., 17.
51. Ibid., 18.
52. Ibid., 19.
53. Ibid., 20.
54. Ibid.
55. Ibid., 21.
56. Ibid., 24.
57. Ibid.
58. Ibid., 29.
59. Ibid.
60. Ibid.
61. Ibid.
62. Ibid.
63. See Emily-Grace Murray, "100Years of Memories: A Personal History of Vae Tancredi," *Reflections: The Newsletter of The Hershey Derry Township Historical Society*, Vol. 22, no.2 (Jan. Feb. March), 2015, 3.
64. Ibid., 4.
65. Murray, "100 Years of Memories: A Personal History of Vae Tancredi," *Reflections: The Newsletter of The Hershey Derry Township Historical Society,"* 2015, 3.
66. See James D. McMahon, *Built on Chocolate: The Story of the Hershey Chocolate Company,* Hershey Foods Corporation, 1998, 3.
67. Murray, "100 Years of Memoires: A Personal History of Vae Tancredi," *Reflections: The Newsletter of The Hershey Derry Township Historical Society,"* 2015, 3.
68. Ibid.
69. Ibid., 4–5.
70. Ibid.
71. Murray, "100 Years of Memories: A Personal History of Vae Tancredi," *Reflections: The Newsletter of The Hershey Derry Township Historical* Society, 2015, 3.
72. Romanucci-Ross, *To Love the Stranger: The Making of An Anthropologist,* 2012, 13.
73. Ibid., 16–17.
74. Ibid., 3.
75. Ibid., 12.
76. Ibid., 20.
77. Ibid.
78. Ibid., 21.
79. Ibid., 22.
80. Ibid.
81. Ibid. 23.
82. Ibid. 25.
83. Ibid., 29–30.
84. Ibid., 31.
85. Ibid., 31–34.
86. Ibid., 37.
87. Ibid., 38.
88. Ibid., 41.
89. Ibid., 42.
90. Ibid., 43.
91. Ibid., 48.
92. Ibid., 49.
93. Ibid., 80.
94. Ibid.

95. Romanucci-Ross, *To Love the Stranger: The Making of an Anthropologist,* 2015, 65.
96. Ibid.
97. Ibid.
98. Ibid.
99. Ibid., 67.
100. Ibid., 7.
101. Ibid., 68.
102. Ibid.
103. Ibid., 69.
104. Ibid., 70.
105. Ibid., 70.
106. Ibid.
107. Ibid., 71.
108. Ibid., 72.
109. Ibid.
110. Ibid.
111. Ibid., 75.
112. Ibid., 80.
113. Ibid., 85.
114. Ibid., 137.
115. Ibid., 141.
116. Ibid., 143–225.
117. Ibid. Afterword, About the Author.

FIVE

The Effect of Fascist Political Repression and the Manifesto of Race on Selected Prominent Italian and Italian American Jewish Academics

Murder and Flight—Italy's Loss and America's Gain—A Multicultural Narrative

Francis N. Elmi

Multiculturalism is equal respect for various cultures in a society or nation. Widespread support for different cultures is essential to the success of multiculturalism. Loss, tragedy, and disruption can sometimes occur when control rests in a dominant culture that does not support or discriminates against a less powerful culture or any other culture. Power is jealously sought and guarded whether in an authoritarian society or even in a democracy. The United States has been a relatively successful example of multiculturalism for the most part, despite forces which resist it. We are a nation of immigrants and that has been our strength even though there has been opposition to a multicultural society at times continuing into the present.

However, there are many historical examples of the oppression of different cultures in many countries. One notorious example is Fascist Italy's maltreatment of Italian Jews exemplified specifically in this chapter in the lives and careers of Italian Jewish academics and scientists: the Rosselli brothers, Salvador Luria, and Rita Levi-Montalcini. The famed scientist Enrico Fermi was not Jewish but was married to Laura Capon, an Italian Jew. He and Laura Capon escaped persecution by leaving Italy before the Racial Laws had much of an impact. The fate of the Rosselli brothers, Carlo and Nello, both academics and scholars, was tragic. By contrast, Fermi, Luria, and Levi-Montalcini entered the successful multicultural society of mid-twentieth century America.

Prior to the frightening implementation of Mussolini's 1938 Manifesto of Race, Carlo and Nello Rosselli, Italian patriots from a prominent family, experienced discrimination, imprisonment, and death for their adherence to the ideals of justice and liberty as well as for their efforts to undermine the dictatorial regime of Benito Mussolini. They are an inspiration to those of us who believe in freedom of assembly, freedom of expression, personal freedom, social justice, and respect for different cultures in society.

A short time after the martyrdom of the Rosselli brothers, the Racial Laws of the Manifesto of Race were implemented in Italy forcing several outstanding Jewish scientists and Enrico Fermi to leave Italy in order to continue their research in America. One of them was forced to remain in Italy in hiding through the duration of World War II when she too left Italy to pursue her scientific career in America. Enrico Fermi had already been notified of his Nobel Prize in Physics before leaving Italy. In America he later became essential to the birth of the atomic age. After Fermi left Italy, Salvador Luria, who also eventually won a Nobel Prize, left Italy for France and then America to study, teach, and do research in the area of neurobiology. After the war ended, another scientist, Rita Levi-Montalcini, followed Fermi and Luria to America, having spent the war years in hiding while doing research secretly. She too eventually won a Nobel Prize.

Mussolini's Manifesto of Race attacking a minority Jewish cultural group ironically became a significant factor in helping America to become preeminent in science as well as victorious in World War II.

A good example of successful multiculturalism is Italy before Mussolini's ascent to power. A specific example is the village where my father was born, Pitigliano, in the Maremma region of southern Tuscany where a large population of Jewish refugees from Papal discrimination in the sixteenth century lived and prospered amidst their neighbors, Italian Christians. The Jews and the Christians lived in close proximity in Pitigliano because it was a small village, and their relationships were harmonious. Pitigliano was somewhat unique since Jews were allowed to own property not only within their ghetto but outside as well. Some even intermarried with the Christian population. Giuseppe Celata's *The Jews of Pitigliano: Four Centuries of a Diverse Community* reports that in 1799,

> people came down to Pitigliano from Orvieto . . . with bad intentions, to loot the shops of the Jews, and to hurt people. However, when the

local townspeople returned from the fields, they defended the Jews with pitch-forks and other tools.[1]

Celata also presents a portrait of the amicable Christian-Jewish relationship which was condemned by Bishop Tancredi: "the familiarity that the Christian children had with Jewish children, so intense, he claims, that both 'males and females follow Jewish children to the Jewish schools'."[2] Celata also stated that despite prohibitions, "Christian women went to the ghetto to breast feed Jewish babies and . . . Jewish wet nurses . . . gave milk to Christian babies."[3] Also, Christians danced and played with Jews. Even Catholic priests "who had an interest in learning frequented homes where Jewish children received their instruction," despite episcopal prohibitions.[4] In 1820 during Austrian rule, the Jews in Pitigliano were given legal equality with Christians; also the Grand Duke approved the "Charter for the Israelite University of Pitigliano" with "full acceptance in peaceful co-existence."[5] In fact, Pitigliano became known as "La Piccola Gersualemme, " and had a thriving synagogue, kosher bath, and kosher bakery, all of which have been restored and now comprise the Jewish Museum today. The presence of a Jewish school and university in Pitigliano served to enlighten not only the Jewish population but the Christian as well. These institutions encouraged political activism during the Risorgimento which culminated in the unification of Italy and the formation of the Italian nation. This activism was transported eventually in the twentieth century by Pitiglianese immigrant families to Hershey, Pennsylvania, where so many of them settled.

Italian Jews in Pitigliano had a significant influence on the cuisine of the village as reflected in the shared recipes of Jews and Christians in a book written by Edda Servi Machlin, a descendant of the most prominent Jewish family in Pitigliano, the Servis, and who was honored here in the United States on her birthday celebrated by the Italian Americans in Hershey, Pennsylvania. The book is entitled *The Classic Cuisine of the Italian Jews*. It is also a "memoir of a vanished way of life" in Pitigliano.[6] Servi Machlin stated that Pitigliano "offered a guarantee of freedom and peaceful cohabitation with the Gentiles"—at least before Mussolini's Racial Laws were implemented.[7] Servi Machlin noted that the Jews "also influenced their Gentile neighbors in food and eating habits and even in the superstitions that went along with them."[8]

This centuries-long connection between Jews and Christians was abruptly disrupted in Pitigliano when Mussolini instituted the Racial Laws as he allied himself with Hitler. Servi Machlin escaped and joined the partisans, but her parents and her younger brother were placed in a concentration camp but managed to remain alive and survive. However, as a result of the war and the flight of Jews from Pitigliano, along with the damage to the temple, the school, the yeshiva, the libraries and the bakery, Jewish life in Pitigliano came to an end.[9] Servi Machlin laments:

"that glorious chapter of human history, the Jewish experience in Pitiglia-no, lives on only in our memories and in our hearts."[10]

However, memory is important. Both in America and Italy, the Pitigli-anese still remember that their paisani during World War II hid their Jewish friends in the Etruscan caves beneath the village until the Germans left. According to Rosina and Francesco Elmi, as well as Clelia Paioletti Brizzi in many conversations with this writer, the Christian Piti-glianese provided food for their Jewish compatriots through secret passageways down to the caves to keep them alive. In recent years, Jews and Christians throughout Europe and even from the United States visit the Jewish Museum which stands as a memorial to the beauty of a multicultural society in Italy. Unfortunately, because of twenty-first century terrorism, Italian soldiers are stationed at the street leading to the museum to prevent anti-Semitic attacks.

The history of Jews in Italy extends back for more than a thousand years as noted by Tobias Jones in his study *The Dark Heart of Italy.* He emphasized that: "Italy has always been pluralistic. The oldest Jewish community in Europe established in 161 B.C. is in Rome."[11] For centuries Jews made significant contributions to Italy, Jones stated, including more recently, "especially their contributions to the literary renaissance in Turin in the postwar years."[12] Turin was also where the aforementioned Salvador Luria and Rita Levi-Montalcini once lived.

The contributions of Italian Jews can be seen in reading Caroline Moorhead's account of the tragic story of an Italian Jewish family's experiences which predated the 1938 imposition of the Manifesto of Race. The attack on two famous Italian Jewish academics was astonishing and horrifying. Moorhead depicts the story of the Rossellis, Italian Jews, and descendants of Sephardic Jews who had fled the Spanish Inquisition in 1492 and who bravely opposed a modern secular inquisition by Mussolini. The Rosselli family was well known for their historical prominence and their social and academic contributions. In the nineteenth century their ancestors supported and protected Mazzini in the liberation of Italy from foreign and Papal rule. The Rossellis were patriotic Italians who had no interest in Zionism. For them, their country was Italy, and their Jewish faith was their religion. In general, most Italian Jews before and during the Mussolini era considered themselves as simply Italians, co-existing peacefully with Christian Italians.

In the second decade of the twentieth century, however, the Rosselli family opposed the dictatorial brutality of Mussolini's regime. Amelia, the matriarch of the family, and her sons, Carlo and Nello, were horrified by the murder of Giacomo Matteoti, who in 1924 had made a stirring speech criticizing the Fascist regime in the Chamber of Deputies of the Italian Parliament. The regime was using "murder, beatings, arson, destruction of homes of left-wing opponents, and forcible administration of castor oil," according to Moorhead.[13] Matteoti's speech was the catalyst for his murder, and this led to the Rossellis' implacable enmity for the Fascist regime and Mussolini. Their opposition to the regime proved to be prescient, for the brutality of Matteoti's murder foreshadowed the undermining of democracy and freedom in Italy, setting the stage for more than two decades of oppressive rule, as well as ruinous wars, and the blood bath resulting from an alliance with Hitler, and the invasion and defeat of Italy in World War II—accompanied by chaos and deprivation for the Italian people.

The Rossellis were open in their opposition to the Mussolini regime and suffered greatly. The fate of Carlo and Nello, both academics, foreshadowed the plight of Italian Jewish scientists in the late 1930s. Amelia Rosselli, a great Italian patriot, was a famous playwright and a pioneering feminist. She eventually became a delegate to the National Congress of Italian Women in Rome.[14] She lost her oldest son, Aldo, in the Dolomite Mountains during World War I.[15] This event caused the younger brothers of Aldo to become intensely patriotic, and both Carlo and Nello entered the military as well. Despite their postwar anti-Fascist, anti-Mussolini sentiments, their loyalty to their country cannot be questioned. Both Carlo and Nello became academics. Carlo wrote a thesis on contemporary socialism, and Nello focused his studies on Mazzini.[16] They both became increasingly involved with politics. Carlo and Nello also created a children's library in a less wealthy area of Florence, an example of their concern for others.[17] The Rosselli brothers also became members of the Circolo di Cultura in Florence, where political and philosophical debates occurred simultaneous with the rise of Mussolini in the early 1920s. After completing his thesis, Carlo studied in London and became increasingly disturbed by Mussolini's bombing of the island of Corfu to resolve a border dispute. A noteworthy event occurred when Nello made a speech at the Jewish Convention in Livorno declaring his Jewishness while asserting at the same time that he felt "profoundly Italian."[18] Nello declared his Jewish faith:

> I call myself Jewish. I hold to my Jewishness . . . because with Jewish severity on the duties of our life on earth, and with Jewish serenity on the mystery of the after-life, because I love all men as in Israel we are commanded to love them . . . because I have the clearest sense of personal responsibility . . . because I have religious commitment to family which all those who look at us from outside agree is a fundamental, adamantine characteristic of Jewish society, I am thus, —I believe a Jew.[19]

As a patriotic Italian, Nello also thus asserted his belief in the moral tenets of his faith. The existence of patriotic Italian Jews belies the commonly held stereotype that being Italian and being Catholic are synonymous.

In 1924 the government abolished the Circolo di Cultura, the Rosselli bastion of democracy in Florence, which "was ransacked."[20] A wave of fascist destruction and agitation swept through Florence. The Rossellis then helped to found *Non Mollare,* (Don't Give Up), an anti-fascist, pro-socialist newspaper. This infuriated the fascists. The Rosselli home was raided and the furniture and other valuables left damaged or destroyed. Throughout this period of turmoil, *Non Mollare* continued to be published and passed around by hand to avoid fascist detection. The Rossellis then moved to Genoa. There they participated in developing the magazine *Il Quarto Stato* (The Fourth Estate) in 1926.[21] Carlo Rosselli and Ferruccio Parri became involved in successfully assisting the escape of Filippo Turati, the leader of the Italian Socialist Party by spiriting him off to Corsica. Upon return to Italy, Carlo was arrested and imprisoned in Forte di Massa near Carrara, and he was later moved to a prison in Como. Meanwhile, Nello had "won a competition for the best thesis in modern history at the prestigious Scuola di Storia Moderna e Contemporanea in Rome, one of the few remaining liberal institutions."[22] Carlo was eventually sent to the penal island of Ustica, and later Nello was sent there as well. In the 1927 trial known as the Trial of the Professors—those who helped Filippo Turati escape—Carlo had been sentenced. Meanwhile Turati, who was living in Paris by this time, sent a letter to the court describing Italy as "one vast Prison."[23] Carlo spoke of Turati thus: "It was only fitting, he said, that he, Carlo, the descendant of a Rosselli who had hidden Mazzini when he fled from his persecutors in the nineteenth century should save another hero of similar moral stature from 'fascist fury.'"[24] The sentence rendered by the judge was that Carlo and his colleagues should spend ten months in prison.[25] Ultimately, Carlo was sent to the penal island of Lipari from which he cleverly escaped and went to Tunis. From there he went to France. It was on Lipari that Carlo began writing his book *Liberal Socialism.*

Nello was punished by being sent to the penal island of Ponza near Naples; however, he was freed through political intervention. Carlo had become so famous for his courage and bold escape that he was "admired by every anti-fascist of every political persuasion and one to be still more hated and feared by Mussolini."[26]

Carlo joined other refugees in Paris where the French treated them well: "there were said to be some 150,000 Italians living in and around Paris at the end of the 1920s and over a million across the whole of France."[27] However, the refugees were in danger of assassination so they did not feel safe even in France. Carlo's celebrity carried him to London where he made speeches. He also plotted with other anti-fascists to make trouble and undermine Mussolini using the anti-fascist movement Giustizia and Liberta (Justice and Liberty) to do so. From Switzerland, for example, Carlo helped organize a leaflet drop that "caused a sensation in Milan."[28] Moorhead describes Mussolini as:

Deeply ambivalent about the Italian intellectuals (like Carlo and Nello), he wanted their imprimatur, but he also feared their dissidence. He preferred them to be inside Italy where they could be watched and threatened rather than abroad where . . . they could mount campaigns against him.[29]

By 1931 Nello found that "Italian academia was now closed to him."[30] This was an example of the punishment Mussolini's regime could render to dissenting academics and scholars.

In Paris the publication of Carlo's book, *Socialisme Liberal* aroused opposition not only among fascists but also communists because he opposed authoritarianism and disagreed with Stalinism. For example, Togliatti, a prominent Italian communist, opposed Carlo Rosselli's promotion of liberal socialism.

Stanislao Pugliese in his biography of Carlo Rosselli interprets socialism "as the aspiration of the people to affirm themselves in history and to participate in the historical process as active protagonists . . . "perpetual becoming," . . . "Infinite progress," and . . . "perpetual striving."[31] Pugliese sees Rosselli's view of socialism "as the extension of political freedom and social justice to the working classes based on the liberal method."[32] Liberalism, according to Rosselli was "the free play of economic forces "as quoted by Pugliese in Gobetti's journal, *La Rivoluzione Liberale.*[33] Pugliese discusses the need for workers to construct a defense against an oligarchy that could develop in moving to control economic life as a result of their freedom to control the means of production.[34] Thus, liberalism needed to be checked so that workers were not exploited. It was therefore necessary to create "the best defense of the consumer [which] can be reached only through their condition as producers."[35] Therefore, the only solution for the working class in a liberal capitalistic society is to organize and become protagonists in the process because of their strength and unity as producers as well as consumers.[36]

According to Pugliese, in France Carlo Rosselli became "the driving force" for the Giustizia e Liberta movement thus threatening the Fascist state in Italy since Carlo traveled extensively in Europe to publicize it as the "essence" of "antifascism."[37] As a revolutionary anti-fascist movement, Giustizia e Liberta fought to end the Fascist dictatorship in Italy, called on Italians to participate in the battle, supported the interests of the working class to achieve social and economic, progress, guaranteed "judicial equality and political liberty" and, as a result, would create through great struggle and sacrifice a much desired objective: "the Second Italian Risorgimento."[38]

Unfortunately, this outcome was not to be. Instead, in Italy many independent-minded teachers and university professors had "to sign an oath of fealty to the king and the fascist regime."[39] Moorhead stated that "The academic world throughout Europe protested loudly and in Lon-

don a letter was published comparing the fascists to the Ku Klux Klan."[40]
The women's movement in Italy came to a halt. Any erotic behavior was
curbed and even Christmas trees were outlawed as they reflected Northern European culture rather than strictly Italian culture.

Carlo became inspired by the Spanish Civil War. He became the most
prominent anti-fascist in exile. He sent money to help the anti-fascist
forces in Spain. He even went to Spain, joined the fighting and was
wounded and almost killed. He sent a radio message to Italy: "Free men,
rise up! Today in Spain, tomorrow in Italy."[41] Later, he returned to Paris
enjoying his celebrity for having been wounded in his heroic efforts to
combat Fascism in the Spanish Civil War. Meanwhile in Rome plans were
afoot to assassinate both Carlo and Nello who were experiencing a happy
reunion in France. Tragically, on June 9, 1937, the two Rosselli brothers
were assassinated by French right-wing fascists at the behest of Mussolini.[42] Moorhead's comment about the Spanish Civil War was poignant: "It
was in some ways a relief that Carlo had not lived to see his friends
reduced to murderous in-fighting and the Republic fail to transform the
Spanish Civil War into a global crusade against fascism."[43] Carlo and
Nello were given a great public funeral in Paris celebrating the sacrifices
they had made in their fight to liberate Italy. In the following year, unfortunately, the Manifesto of Race was instituted in Italy to eliminate or limit
severely the presence and contributions of Italian Jews to Italian
  society and specifically to their academic and scientific pursuits—an
eventual great loss to Italy. Hitler's malign anti-Semitic influence was
officially manifest in Mussolini's Italy.

By 1938, the Manifesto of Race was in effect officially in Italy. Christopher Duggan's *The Force of Destiny. A History of Italy since 1796* noted that
Mussolini alleged that eighty percent of Bolshevik leaders "were Jews
operating in the service of Jewish banks in London and New York."[44]
This statement illustrates Mussolini's fear of the far left as well as his
construction of a reason to instill fear of Jewish influence in Italy. Duggan
further stated that Africans also were a target of Mussolini's racist poli-
cies: "A decree of April 1937 made it a crime, punishable with up to five
years in prison, for a citizen to have a conjugal relationship with an
African subject."[45] According to Duggan, prior to 1937, Mussolini did not
consider Jews in Italy to be a problem. Representation in the Fascist Party
included many Italian Jews in high positions including, ironically, Mussolini's own Jewish mistress, Margahrita Sarfarti.[46]

The Manifesto of Race stipulated the following prohibitions and rules
regarding Jewish Italians according to Clough and Saladino's *A History of
Modern Italy, Documents, Reading, and Commentary*:

> Jews were prohibited from marrying a person of a different race. Even
> if a person belongs to a religion "other than Jewish" if that person has
> Jewish parents, he or she is Jewish. This applies to a person born to a

Jewish mother but whose father is unknown and to a person of Italian nationality but has only one parent who is Jewish. Any person who is Jewish must be publicly registered as Jewish. Italian Jews may not be part of the military or be involved in defense industry, nor be involved in enterprises of more than 199 persons. Jewish children may be removed from parental authority if they follow a religion other than Jewish while the parent is educating them in a manner not in keeping with their chosen faith or not in accordance with national principles. Jews may not be employed by the government, the Fascist Party, municipal government, national banks or insurance companies. No foreign Jews can reside in Italy, Libya or Aegean possessions of Italy. Jewish employees of the government, the Fascist Party, and insurance companies will be terminated in three months after this decree is promulgated. Foreign Jews who have become citizens after January 1, 1919, will have their citizenship rescinded. [47]

In addition, according to Denis Mack Smith's *Modern Italy: A Political History*, "certain books were prohibited including the great literary treasures of Machiavelli and Boccaccio." [48] Smith added:

> Jews could not become journalists, teachers, or notaries; recent immigrants were to be expelled. Jews could not attend state schools; they could not go to the university or possess telephone numbers, and some of their property was forfeit. [49]

Larry Hartensian in his biography of Mussolini, *Benito Mussolini*, noted significantly that "after Hitler's visit in 1938, a new kind of racist thinking emerged in Italy: anti-Semitism." [50] As late as the early 1930s, "Mussolini had scoffed at Hitler's anti-Semitism," according to Hartensian who noted that "only one tenth of one percent of the population" were Jewish. [51] Obviously, by 1938, Mussolini wanted to prove his loyalty to his indispensable friend and ally, Adolf Hitler, as he instituted laws that would disrupt, ruin, and in many cases, end the lives of Italian Jews.

The Manifesto of Race had an intimidating effect on prominent Italian scientists including Enrico Fermi, Salvador Luria, and Rita Levi-Montalcini. Fermi, although not Jewish himself, was worried about the fate of his Jewish wife, Laura Capon, and his children who were in danger. He also felt that his brilliant career was threatened. As a child and young boy, he became interested in science, particularly physics. Ultimately, he studied at the Scuola Normale Superiore in Pisa where he excelled in physics, and within a short time he was publishing papers in physics and received his "magna cum laude doctorate," at the early age of twenty in July 1922. [52] Fermi wrote a paper on Einstein's theory of relativity while only a student in Pisa; Fermi is described as "one of the very few at the time who emphasized its importance." [53] He went on to study at German universities, was given a fellowship by the Rockefeller Foundation, became a professor at the University of Florence and lectured at the prestigious Sapienza University of Rome. His statistical formulation led to the development of the Fermi-Dirac statistics.[54]

Fermi married Laura Capon in 1928 after he became a professor at the Sapienza University of Rome. He even became a member of the Fascist Party after being appointed to the Royal Academy of Italy in 1929. Later, in the United States, his affiliation with the Fascist Party aroused suspicion in the FBI, but "Those who knew him, who knew how lucky the United States was to have him on the side of the Allies, had no doubts about his loyalty."[55] Fermi continued his work in Italy before leaving, making many discoveries in physics, particularly nuclear physics, with significant implications for his future. Fermi was awarded the Nobel Prize in 1938, the same year as the imposition of the Manifesto of Race. 1938 became a turning point in Fermi's life, for he was married to an Italian Jew, and therefore his life in Italy was to be disrupted. He planned to leave for America with his wife and children.

Fermi had been considering emigration for several years in order to explore further research and funding in the United States where he had already taught. In 1938 he secretly accepted an offer from Columbia University because he feared the effects of the Manifesto of Race, the draconian Racial Laws, on his wife and children. According to Schwartz's biography of Fermi, on November 10, 1938, Fermi received a call from Sweden informing him that he had won the Nobel Prize in Physics.[56] Fermi's work on "slow neutrons and the discovery of transuranic elements" was the basis of his Nobel award.[57] A passport issue complicated the Fermi family's departure for Sweden. Since Laura was Jewish she could encounter difficulty in entering Germany on the way to Sweden.[58] Therefore, she converted to Catholicism; her children were already Catholic. The Fermis underwent a second marriage ceremony as Catholics, which was cleverly pre-dated.[59] These short-term subterfuges enabled them to travel to Sweden. Afterwards, Fermi and his family traveled to Denmark and England, setting sail for New York from Southampton on December 24, 1938.[60] From that moment on, Italy had lost a great scientist whose work in America would change the world.

Laura Capon Fermi loved Rome and did not want to leave Italy. However, the anti-Semitic conditions in Italy and Germany not only might have affected herself but her children since Jews had been defined as a separate race from Christian Italians whether they were converts to Catholicism or not. In addition, Laura "was also familiar with German racial laws that defined children with a Jewish mother as Jewish."[61] There was no choice. The Fermis had to leave Italy and find refuge and a new life in America.

Within months of his arrival in the United States, Fermi's reputation and work ethic served him well. He began teaching at Columbia University. He commenced research on nuclear fusion and "wrote forty-seven papers describing the experimental work leading to the creation of the world's first controlled self-sustaining chain reaction on December 2, 1942."[62] He worked on the Manhattan Project which became the Atomic Energy Commission in 1947. He was also instrumental in developing nuclear power and the hydrogen bomb. His work led to the application of nuclear weapons to war before the Germans were able to and this enabled America and its allies to be victorious in World War II. He spent his later years teaching and died at age 53. In addition to the Nobel Prize, he won many other prizes but valued one in particular:

> Among all these tributes he would be most proud of the prize bearing his name that the USAEC (United States Atomic Energy Commission) awards annually, first granted Fermi on his death bed. . . . The Enrico Fermi Award . . . to encourage excellence in research in energy science and technology benefiting mankind."[63]

After the war, when democracy was restored, Italians gave Fermi's name to streets, piazzas, train stations and other facilities.[64] And he is remembered fondly in his native land.

Salvador Luria, another great scientist and friend to Fermi, was an Italian Sephardic Jew who, like Enrico Fermi and his family, left Italy in 1938. In his autobiography, *A Slot Machine, A Broken Test Tube,* Luria, who at the time of his departure from Italy, was a medical doctor, stated that on July 17, 1938, the day before the Manifesto of Race was proclaimed by Mussolini, he had received word that his Italian fellowship at the University of California at Berkley had been approved.[65] Logically, Luria considered the Manifesto of Race to be "especially preposterous because Italy was undoubtedly the least anti-Semitic of European countries."[66] He supported this statement by noting that there were very few Jews in Italy and that there had been prominent patriotic Jews in the Risorgimento as well as in the government. Luria seemed astounded at the imposition of the Racial Laws. Soon, as a medical doctor, Luria himself was investigated by the Fascist government for his disobedience in having worked as "an assistant (without pay) in a few hospital departments."[67] Luria realized that he could no longer pursue his Italian fellowship in California as a result of the Racial Laws. Despite these problems, Luria knew that the Italian people as a rule, but with some exceptions, were not anti-Semitic. He noted that Gentile Italians trusted their Jewish compatriots: "the Italian people, including the police and soldiers, tried, often successfully to save the Jews from deportation."[68]

However, news from Germany regarding Kristallnacht "meant that the persecution of Jews was not likely, even in Italy, to remain merely non-violent humiliation."[69] Because of the threat of violence against Jews, Luria decided not to return to the medical profession and to leave Italy to pursue a career in science. He had already developed an interest in biophysics and was planning a life in scientific research rather than medicine even before the Manifesto of Race was imposed. As far back as 1927,

Fermi had agreed to have Luria study radiology and physics at the University of Rome after he left the military. Luria wanted to continue the research he had already begun in Italy involving Max Delbruck's formulation of the concept of gene as molecule.[70] Meanwhile, Luria's family had lost their business, and his brother had lost his job as a result of the Manifesto of Race.[71] Therefore, he decided to leave Italy for Paris, realizing that Enrico Fermi with his Jewish wife and family had left "for Stockholm to receive the Nobel Prize and thence for New York."[72] Luria did research in France, but as a result of the German invasion of Belgium and Holland, in May 1940 he went to Marseille to obtain a visa to apply for American citizenship. He then left Europe on a Greek ship sailing from Lisbon and arrived in the United States on September 12, 1943.[73]

In New York Luria visited Enrico Fermi who recommended him for a position at the Rockefeller Foundation; thus, with several mini-fellowships, Luria began research at the College of Physicians and Surgeons of Columbia University.[74] Luria also worked with Max Delbruck, a refugee from Nazi Germany, at the Biological Laboratory of Cold Spring Harbor, a center for the study of genetics and molecular biology. There they discovered "that...if two different phages attacked the same bacterium only one of them could multiply..."[75] (A phage is a bacteria-destroying agent.) This experiment "proved to have a seminal role in the rise of molecular biology. "[76] This was an important discovery in the nature and explanation of bacterial viruses and aroused the "interest evinced by specialists in viral diseases."[77] Luria was also awarded a Guggenheim Fellowship at Vanderbilt University where he continued working with Max Delbruck; however, by 1943 he was offered an instructorship at Indiana University in Bloomington, Indiana.[78] It is there that Luria realized "the analogy between slot-machine returns and clusters of mutant bacteria" while observing slot machines at a faculty dance.[79] This led to further experiments that resulted in the discovery that "resistant bacteria originated by spontaneous mutation," a major step in genetics, mutations which "caused bacteria to become resistant to antibiotics such as penicillin or streptomycin."[80] This research emphasized the importance of bacterial genetics, biochemistry and physics in solving health problems.

While teaching at Indiana University, Luria taught many fine students, one of whom, his first student, James Watson, eventually won a Nobel Prize by discovering the structure of DNA. Another of Luria's students was from Italy, Renato Dulbecco, who went on to receive a Nobel Prize as a result of his work on viruses and tumor cells at Cal Tech. Alfred Hershey, whom Luria knew at both Vanderbilt University and Indiana University, eventually shared the Nobel Prize in 1969 with both Luria and Max Delbruck.[81] Luria not only contributed his own expertise to his work in bacterial genetics but also influenced other students and colleagues to excel and create major progress in improving human health.

After leaving Indiana University because the administration was upset with his 1945 Progressive Party affiliations and union organizing, Luria taught at the University of Illinois at Champagne-Urbana where he continued his study of bacterial viruses, genetics, and molecular biology.[82]

By 1958, Luria was offered a position at the Massachusetts Institute of Technology where he concentrated "on building the Biology Department into one of the best in the world."[83] Luria also studied at the Pasteur Institute in Paris where he began to focus on membrane-active proteins since "Biologists from all over the world were in Paris, exploring the implications of the new theory ('the operon Theory, a powerful model of gene regulation')."[84] While at M.I.T. in the late 60s, Luria became a political activist opposing the Vietnam War, and in 1969 he was awarded the Nobel Prize in Physiology or Medicine. In his autobiography, Luria emphasized in particular the statement made by Alfred Hershey at the Nobel banquet in Stockholm: "You are working for knowledge and the good of mankind. God bless you."[85] Also, in 1969, Luria received the Luisa Horvitz Prize of Columbia University which he shared with Max Delbruck.[86] Luria's leadership role at The Cancer Center at M.I.T. led to efficacious work on tumor viruses for which three of his colleagues, David Baltimore, Renato Dulbecco, and Howard Temin were awarded the Nobel Prize.[87]

Because of freedom of expression in the United States, Luria was free to criticize the American government without fear. His strong voice against the Vietnam War is an example. As we now know his opposition to the war was justified. This freedom also led him to explore knowledge with beneficial results in the field of medicine.

As we have seen, Luria also had the ability to attract other scientists with whom he collaborated. While teaching at Indiana University, Luria promoted the immigration of Rita Levi-Montalcini whom he knew years before in Italy at the University of Turin. He considered her "a great neurobiologist, collector of honors and prizes as well as the nickname 'the queen' because of her impeccable dresses and regal manner."[88] She too had been a victim of the Manifesto of Race, hiding in Italy during World War II while secretly continuing her research. Levi-Montalcini—at the recommendation of Luria—began teaching at Washington University in St. Louis full-time in 1947 after finishing a fellowship there, joining Professor Hamberger, a Jewish refugee from Nazi Germany, in advancing the study of the Nerve Growth Factor along with Stanley Cohen, a biochemist.

Like Luria, Rita Levi-Montalcini was a Sephardic Jew who lived and studied in Turin. She was born into a relatively affluent family. In her autobiography, *In Praise of Imperfection*, Levi-Montalcini expressed her disinterest in conforming to the Victorian model of womanhood—to marry and have children. Instead, she developed an interest in becoming a doctor as a result of seeing her beloved governess, Giovanna, die of stomach cancer.[89] In medical school at the University of Turin, she studied with Giuseppe Levi, and became interested in the important process of the development of the nervous system. According to *10 Women who changed Science and the World,* by Catherine Whitlock and Rhodri Evans, Levi-Montalcini focused on "the development and function of neurons . . . highlighted by diseases such as Alzheimer's and Parkinson's which are caused by damage to brain neurons."[90] In her autobiography Levi-Montalcini wrote that she was a free thinker who was raised as a secular Jew; therefore, she had no definite thoughts about religion: "Was I Jewish, Israelite, or devil knows what else?"[91] She did not attend synagogue or church.[92] The Levi family did observe the Passover celebration, but other Jewish celebrations "particularly highlighted discomfort."[93] Her father, also a secular Jew, informed his children that they were exempt from Yom Kippur whereas her cousins had to fast and atone for their sins.[94] Whitlock and Evans report that "Rita (formerly Levi) distinguished herself from the other intellectual Jews of Turin by changing her name to Levi-Montalcini," an example of her rebellion against becoming "the traditional Italian wife and mother."[95]

However, as anti-Semitism gradually took hold in Italy, Levi-Montalcini's free-thinking secular status no longer mattered, for Italy had transformed from being "a tolerant country of liberal teaching" in which Jews had been liberated from second-class treatment "into the vassal of Nazi Germany."[96] As a result, Levi-Montalcini wrote of her feelings at the time:

> For the first time I felt pride in being Jewish and not Israelite, as we had been customarily called in the liberal climate of my early years. And though still profoundly secular, I felt a bond with those who were, like me, the victims of the lurid campaign unleashed by the Fascist press."[97]

By 1939, Levi-Montalcini could no longer attend university activities as a result of the imposition of the Racial Laws. She decided to go to Brussels to work and study in a neurological institute with her mentor Giuseppe Levi.[98] However, as the war threatened Belgium she decided to return to Italy hoping to evade a German invasion.[99] When Mussolini's alliance with Hitler became official, hopes for peace evaporated.[100] Meanwhile, upon returning to Italy, Levi-Montalcini began practicing medicine secretly, visiting the poor and administering medical care; however, she could not continue because prescriptions had to be signed by "Aryan" doctors.[101] Levi-Montalcini had already developed an intense interest in studying the nervous system. Secretly, she created a laboratory in her bedroom, but ultimately she had to leave Turin to travel to the Piedmont highlands to continue her studies and experiments there in a farmhouse. By 1942 she left northern Italy for Florence since the war was threatening to disrupt life there. There she once again hid and did research secretly until the Allies became successful in Italy. The Allied forces pushed the Germans back and as British troops arrived in Florence, Levi-Montalcini saw "a bus marked with the Star of David—now no longer an object of derision."[102] She spent her time in liberated Florence helping the Allies with the medical care of war refugees since an epidemic of typhoid had broken out.[103] Returning to Turin, she commenced her research again.

Very soon thereafter, Levi-Montalcini began communicating with Salvador Luria, then at Indiana University, who encouraged her to depart for America to pursue her research. In 1946, Giuseppe Levi informed her that she had been invited to continue her neuroembryological work at Washington University in St. Louis, Missouri. She left for the United States on September 19, 1946.[104] After her semester fellowship ended, Levi-Montalcini was offered a full-time research position at Washington University. She remained there for thirty years while eventually also serving as the director of the Laboratory for Cell Biology in Rome.[105] Levi-Montalcini worked first in American laboratories and later in Italy. Her work was honored when she received the Nobel Prize in Physiology or Medicine which she shared with her long-time associate, Stanley Cohen in 1986.[106] Study of the Nerve Growth Factor developed therapies for diseases that can slow down "the degeneration of the nervous system."[107] Her work also focused on the biology of cancer. Levi-Montalcini kept active throughout her retirement years until her death in 2012 at the age of 103. In 2001 the President of Italy appointed her Senator for Life in the Italian Senate to acknowledge her contributions to science in a democratic Italy.[108] Levi-Montalcini set an example for women around the world to make contributions to science. Not even the threat of imprisonment or death could stop her from doing research in wartime Italy. Her achievements during the war in Italy led to her great success in academe and science in America. When Italy became once again a democracy and returned to its respect for a multicultural society, Levi-Montalcini also contributed to scientific success in her native land.

All the risks she had taken after 1938 and during World War II in Italy, along with her devotion to science in America and later again in Italy, had borne fruit in advances in neurobiology giving impetus to scientists today in working to find therapies and potentially a cure for Alzheimer's, Parkinson's and other diseases of the nervous system.

The multicultural society here in America liberated Italian Jewish scientists as well as Enrico Fermi to do their research for the benefit of humanity. Here in America their research was unimpeded. These experiences of Italian Jewish scientists during the Mussolini and World War II years are a lesson to be learned and taken seriously. Their experiences in immigration and their work illustrate the value newcomers to the United States can make. Freedom to study and work in America create contributions to human knowledge and improvements in human health which should not be impeded by bigotry and fear. The sacrifices of the Rosselli brothers dramatized the fortitude needed to combat Fascism. Their fate and example led Fermi, Luria and Levi-Montalcini to flourish in America and to restore honor to their native land, which was freed from Fascism and is now a democracy.

But today more than ever, vigilance and hard work are needed to maintain freedom of thought, important scientific research, and freedom of expression in both countries — the United States and Italy.

Those who believe in multiculturalism are pluralists as David Brooks recently wrote in an editorial in *The New York Times:*

> Pluralists believe that culture mixing has always been and should be the human condition. All cultures define and renew themselves through encounter. A pure culture is a dead culture while an amalgam culture is a creative culture. [109]

The benefit of this amalgam can be seen in the lives of the Rosselli brothers, Fermi, Luria, and Levi-Montalcini.

Multiculturalism defines the United States. From the very beginning of its existence America has been a successful example of multiculturalism. The great American poet Walt Whitman wrote poetry which became a paean to a multicultural America in these lines from his poem, "By Blue Ontario's Shore."

> Here is not a nation but a Nation of nations . . .
> Here the flowing trains, here the crowds, equality,
> Diversity, the soul loves. [110]

We must always remember, however, that even in America, the land of immigrants, multiculturalism and diversity succeeded despite numerous attempts to maintain the dominance of an Anglo-Saxon white nation. The title of a recent study of immigration in America reveals the nature of those attempts quite succinctly: *The Guarded Gate: Bigotry, Eugenics, and the Law That Kept Two Generations of Jews, Italians, and Other European Immigrants Out of America* by Daniel Okrent. This law is the Johnson-Reed Act of 1924. Harshly limiting immigration, national quota systems were imposed. Enrico Fermi, Salvador Luria and Rita Levi-Montalcini were fortunate because of their educational qualifications, academic connections, and scientific expertise. They could and did emigrate to contribute greatly to American success. However, those Jews and Italians who were barred from entering the United States for two generations suffered deprivation, and in the case of millions of Jews and many Italians, mass execution under Fascist and Nazi regimes. The Johnson-Reed Act was in effect until 1965 when President Lyndon Johnson signed the Immigration and Nationality Act that abolished the quotas limiting immigration and put into place a nationality-neutral immigration system. [111]

We can only hope that continued multicultural benefits and success arise from new immigrants today in America as well as in Italy and throughout Europe—despite current attempts to achieve the opposite.

NOTES

1. Giuseppe Celata, *The Jews of Pitigliano: Four centuries of a Diverse Community*, Pitigliano, Grosseto: N.P., 2001, 127.
2. Ibid.
3. Ibid.
4. Ibid. 72.
5. Ibid. 99.
6. Edda Servi Machlin, *The Classic Cuisine of The Italian Jews: Traditional Recipes and Menus and a Memoir of a Vanished Way of Life*, New York: Dodd, Mead and Company, Inc., 1981.
7. Ibid., 28.
8. Ibid., 30.
9. Ibid., 38.
10. Ibid.
11. Tobias Jones, *The Dark Heart of Italy*, New York: North Point Press, a division of Farrar, Straus, and Giroux, 2017, xiii.
12. Ibid.
13. Caroline Moorhead, *A Bold and Dangerous Family*, New York: Harper Collins Publishers, 2017, xiii.
14. Ibid., 37.
15. Ibid., 57.
16. Ibid., 73.
17. Ibid., 70.
18. Ibid., 124.
19. Ibid., Qtd. in Moorhead, 124.
20. Ibid., 120.
21. Ibid., 125.
22. Ibid., 123.
23. Ibid., 184–185.
24. Ibid.
25. Ibid., 186.
26. Ibid., 187.
27. Ibid., 247.
28. Ibid., 274
29. Ibid.
30. Ibid., 275.
31. Stanislao Pugliese, *Carlo Rosselli: Socialist Heretic and Antifascist Exile*, Cambridge: Harvard University Press, 1999, 53.
32. Ibid., 57–58.
33. Ibid., 47–48. Qtd. in Rosselli's article in Gobetti's journal *La Rivoluzione Liberale*.
34. Ibid., 48.
35. Ibid., 48. Qtd. in "La lotta di classe nel movimento operaio, *Opere scelte*, I, p. 45.
36. Ibid.
37. Ibid., 127.
38. Ibid., quoted in *Giustizia e Liberta*, no.1, November 1929; AGL, sezione IV, fascicolo 2, sotto fascicolo 1, insert 2, no.1.
39. See Caroline Moorhead, *A Bold and Dangerous Family*, Harper Collins Publishers, 275.
40. Ibid., 276.

41. Ibid., 334.

42. Ibid., 343–350.

43. Ibid., 359.

44. Christopher Duggan. *The Force of Destiny. A History of Italy since 1796,* New York: Houghton Mifflin, 2008, 417.

45. Ibid., 511.

46. Ibid., 512.

47. Shepard B. Clough and Salvatore Saladino, *A History of Modern Italy: Documents, Reading and Commentary, New York: Columbia University Press,* 1968, 496.

48. Denis Mack Smith, *Modern Italy: A Political History,* Ann Arbor: The University of Michigan Press, 1997, 361.

49. Ibid., 396.

50. Larry Hartensian, *Benito Mussolini,* New York: Chelsea House Publishers, 1988.

51. Ibid., 83.

52. Gene Segre and Bettina Hoerlin. *The Pope of Physics, Enrico Fermi and the Birth of the Atomic Age,* New York: Picador Henry Holt and Company, 2016, 28.

53. David N. Schwartz. *The Last Man Who Knew Everything; The Life and Times of Enrico Fermi, Father of the Nuclear Age,* New York: Basic Books, 2017, 28.

54. Ibid., 56.

55. Ibid., 189.

56. Ibid., 141.

57. Ibid., 119.

58. Ibid., 141.

59. Ibid.

60. Ibid., 145.

61. See Gino Segre and Bettina Hoerlin. *The Pope of Physics,* Pindar Henry Holt and Company, 118.

62. See Schwartz, *The Last Man Who Knew Everything,* Basic Books, 180.

63. Ibid., 356.

64. Ibid.

65. Salvador Edward Luria. *A Slot Machine, A Broken Test Tube,* New York: Harper and Row Publishers, 1984, 21.

66. Ibid.

67. Ibid.

68. Ibid., 22.

69. Ibid.

70. Ibid., 20.

71. Ibid., 22.

72. Ibid.

73. Ibid., 25–29.

74. Ibid., 31.

75. Ibid., 71.

76. Ibid.

77. Ibid., 72.

78. Ibid., 37.

79. Ibid., 75–79.

80. Ibid., 78–79.

81. Ibid., 43.

82. Ibid., 42–45.

83. Ibid., 46.

84. Ibid. 50.

85. Ibid., 54.

86. Ibid., 53.

87. Ibid., 55.

88. Ibid., 42.

89. Rita Levi-Montalcini, *In Praise of Imperfection, My Life and Work,* Trans. Luigi Attardi, New York; Basic Books, 1988, 38.

90. Catherine Whitlock and Rhodri Evans, *10 Women who changed Science and the World*, New York: Diversion Books, 2019, 167.

91. Rita Levi-Montalcini, *In Praise of Imperfection, My Life and Work,* Basic Books, 1988, 19.

92. Ibid.

93. Ibid., 23.

94. Ibid., 25.

95. Catherine Whitlock and Rhodri Evans, *10 Women who changed Science and the World,* Diversion Books, 2019, 142.

96. Rita Levi-Montalcini, *In Praise of Imperfection, My Life and Work,* Basic Books, 1988, 78.

97. Ibid., 80.

98. Ibid., 85–86.

99. Ibid., 87.

100. Ibid.

101. Ibid. 88.

102. Ibid., 105.

103. Ibid., 106–108.

104. Ibid., 117.

105. Catherine Whitlock and Rhodri Evans, *10 Women who changed Science and the World,* Diversion Books, 2019, 182.

106. Ibid., 184.

107. Ibid., 188.

108. Ibid., 186.

109. David Brooks. "The Ideology of Hate and How to Fight It." Editorial - *The New York Times.* 6 Aug. 2019. A 19.

110. Walt Whitman, *Walt Whitman: The Compete Poems,* Ed. By Francis Murphy, New York; Penguin Group USA, 364–365.

111. Daniel Okrent, *The Guarded Gate: Bigotry, Eugenics, and the Law That Kept Two Generations of Jews, Italians, and Other European Immigrants Out of America,* New York: Scribner, 2019. 394.

SIX

The Holocaust and Italy

A Brief Discussion

Louis J. Gesualdi and Lisa Kuan

Many people and textbooks have discussed the atrocities that the Jews have faced during WWII and the Holocaust but few discuss the triumphs and the kindness of humanity during these times. In this chapter, we will be discussing just that.[1] To begin, Lucy Dawidowicz, in *The War against the Jews,* has studied the Holocaust and the percentage of Jews killed. She states that in Poland, before World War II, there were 3,300,000 Jews, and 3,000,000 (90 percent) were killed; in Germany and Austria as of August 1939 210,000 of 240,000 Jews (88 percent) were killed; in Belgium there were 65,000 Jews before World War II, and 40,000 (60 percent) were killed. In most of Europe, most of the Jews were killed during World War II. However, in Italy there were 40,000 Jews before World War II, and 8,000 (20 percent) were killed.[2] In other words, unlike most of Europe, 80 percent of the Jews in Italy survived the Holocaust. How is this so? What was different in Italy that enabled so many Jews to survive unlike the majority of Europe?

This chapter also discusses Walter Wolff's book *Bad Times Good People: A Holocaust Survivor Recounts His Life in Italy during WWII* and Elizabeth Bettina's book *It Happened in Italy: Untold Stories of How the People Defied the Horrors of the Holocaust.* These two works describe the goodness and kindness of many Italians toward strangers at a time when many other parts of Europe were participating in Hitler's Final Solution.

Walter Wolff is a German Jew who lived through the Holocaust in both Germany and Italy. In his book *Bad Times Good People*, Mr. Wolff describes his life in Germany after Hitler's rise to power. Under Hitler, anti-Semitism and Jewish extinction were official state policy. In November1938, Mr. Wolff was arrested and imprisoned in the Dachau concentration camp. After an incredible escape from Dachau, Mr. Wolff, along with his mother and brother, fled to their freedom in Italy. Unfortunately for Mr. Wolff, in 1943, the Germans occupied northern Italy. Mr. Wolff and his family were then constantly on the move throughout Italy avoiding the Nazis until World War II ended.[3]

Walter Wolff and his family are a segment of a very large group of Jews that survived in Italy during World War II. As, Wolff recalls, this was in part due to the willingness of the Italians to protect Wolff and his family while risking their own lives. Wolff points out that eighty percent of the Italian Jews survived the Holocaust because of those Italians who had the courage to follow their beliefs while helping others.[4] In addition, Mr. Wolfe indicated that at least fifty Italian individuals had helped him and his family escape. This included how the Italians misled the Nazi's in giving directions enabling their escape. His narrative is one of endurance, sensitivity, wisdom, and eventually, victory over the Nazis.

In *It Happened in Italy*, Elizabeth Bettina discovered that her childhood village in Campagna, Italy had a little known secret: over a half century ago. The secret at the time was that many of Campagna's residents risked their own lives to shelter, hide and feed hundreds of Jews during the Holocaust, against the Nazis' will. Bettina uncovered fascinating untold stories of different Jews throughout Italy during World War II and the brave Italians who risked their lives to save them. In fact, there were thousands of Italians sheltering and helping Jews all over Italy.[5]

In conclusion, Walter Wolff's *Bad Times Good People* and Elizabeth Bettina's *It Happened in Italy* should be required reading for all people. Wolff's book and Betttina's book chronicle the refusal of ordinary Italian civilians to participate in Hitler's Final Solution. It also reminds us that human beings can prevail when all hope seems to be lost.

NOTES

1. This chapter, originally an unpublished paper, presented as Louis Gesualdi and Lisa Kuan, "The Holocaust and Italy: A Preliminary Report" at the *Over Five Centuries of Italian American History*, The American Italian Sociohistorical Association Third Conference Series held at the University of Cork, Cork, Ireland (July 28, 2017).

2. See Lucy Dawidowicz, *The War Against the Jews, 1937–1945*, New York: Holt, Rinehart and Winston, 1975.

3. See Walter Wolff, *Bad Times Good People: A Holocaust Survivor Recounts His Life in Italy during WWII*, Long Beach, NY: Whittier, 1998.

4. Ibid.

5. See Elizabeth Bettina, *It Happened in Italy: Untold Stories of How the People Defied the Horrors of the Holocaust*, Nashville, TN: Thomas Nelson Publishers, 2011.

SEVEN

A Brief Discussion on Roseto

Louis J. Gesualdi

This chapter briefly discusses John G. Bruhn and Stewart Wolf's *The Roseto Story: An Anatomy of Health* (1979).[1] Bruhn and Wolf's study (sixteen years of research beginning in the early 1960s) investigates the Italian community of Roseto, Pennsylvania. The book's findings indicate that a close knit community (such as the Italian-American community of Roseto) acts as an area of defense against the effects of stress, bereavement and life changes.[2]

The Roseto Story demonstrates that the traditional community life established in Italy was continued by first and second generation Italian-Americans in Roseto, Pennsylvania. Bruhn and Wolf's study describes how the extended family and social organizations (such as mutual benefit societies, religious organizations and others) kept Roseto a closely knit Italian-American community. The book makes evident that the extended families of Roseto's Italian-Americans provided assistance for their members (that is, caring for sick and elderly members). Moreover, the text points out that the social organizations provided support for the cohesiveness among Italian-Americans in Roseto.[3]

Bruhn and Wolf found that the Italian- American community support systems of Roseto, PA appear to be a major factor in Roseto's lower rate of fatal heart attacks. They indicate that from 1955 to 1961, the death rate from heart attacks in Roseto was less than one third the average in the United States. The authors explain that traditional community life played a key role in the low rate of heart attacks among Roseto Italian-Americans.[4]

Bruhn and Wolf's book shows that younger, college educated Italian-Americans (third generation) from Roseto found Roseto's traditional rules and values of the extended family and social organizations to be incompatible with social mobility and career promotion. The text points out that these college educated Italian-Americans adopted a lifestyle typical of middle-class Americans (that is more individual oriented than group oriented) and became heart attack victims. Furthermore, the text indicates that by the early 1970s, the previously traditional community life was almost non-existent among the grandchildren of the original Italian-Americans of Roseto, and that fatal heart attacks began to occur among young third generation Italian-American men of Roseto for the first time.[5]

The Roseto Story determines that when a close knit community (such as Roseto) no longer provided solid social support, heart attacks among these Italian-Americans increased. Traditional community life had been of great benefit to the physical and mental health of the people of Roseto. In conclusion, Bruhn and Wolf demonstrate the importance of community bonds to good health.[6]

NOTES

1. This chapter was originally published in Louis Gesualdi, *The Italian/American Experience: A Collection of Writings* (Lanham, Maryland: University Press of America, 2012). Also, parts of this chapter was presented in Louis Gesualdi, "Closing Remarks" *The Italian American Experience: A Sociohistorical Examination,* American Italian Sociohistorical Association First Conference Series held at St. John's University, Queens, New York (October 21, 2015).

2. John G. Bruhn and Steward Wolf, *The Roseto Story: An Anatomy of Health,* (Norman, Oklahoma: University of Oklahoma Press, 1979).

3. Ibid.

4. Ibid.

5. Ibid.

6. Ibid.

EIGHT

Popularly Held Beliefs about Italian Americans and Organized Crime

Louis J. Gesualdi

As we begin the third decade of the twenty-first century, as a society, we like to think of our civilization progressing and modernizing; especially through globalization. However, I am disappointed to say that disturbing and popularly held beliefs about Italian Americans and organized crime in the United States still exist. In fact, there is a continually high percentage of Americans who disapprove of this group. Therefore, to examine progress in society, this chapter will examine the stigmas held about Italian Americans and organized crime. Second, this chapter presents data that shows a more accurate depiction of this ethnic group with some recommendations to improve relations with Italian Americans.[1]

One of the reasons for the negative portrayal of Italian Americans can be seen in S. Robert Lichter and Daniel R. Amundon's report *Portrayal of Italian American Characters in Prime Television Series 1994–1995*. These authors show that Italian Americans are rarely seen as heroes or even in a high status role on television. The study also shows evidence of popular culture's continuing association of Italian Americans with organized crime.[2] This can also be seen in Bill Dal Cerro's research *Italian Culture on Film 1928–1999* (1999) which analyzes how Italian Americans are portrayed in movies over a 70-year period. Results of the research reveal a consistent negative portrayal of Italian/Americans (that is 74 percent of the films involving Italian/Americans). What is meant by negative portrayal in popular culture are movies dealing with Italian/Americans, images of Italian/Americans as violent criminals predominate (41 percent), followed by portrayals of boors, buffoons, bigots and other social undesirables (33 percent).[3] Presently, media bias still persists. In 2015 the Italic Institute of America, "Film Study 2015 (1914–2014)" found that almost 70 percent of Italian related films produced from 1914 to 2014 portrayed Italians in a negative light. The Institute also provides a list of more recent media releases that contain negative portrayals of Italians. The list includes cartoons, games, books, television shows, movies and several remakes that turned an unidentified villain into a villain with an Italian surname.[4] These figures clearly indicate an entrenched, institutionalized bias against Americans of Italian descent in the entertainment industry.

The National Public Opinion Research for Commission for Social Justice Order Sons of Italy in America's study *Americans of Italian Descent: A Study of Public Images, Beliefs and Misperceptions* reports that 74 percent of the U.S. public sees Italian Americans associated with organized crime.[5] Richard A. Capozzola's work *Finalmente: The Truth about Organized Crime* suggests that the media and politicians, by exaggerating the role of Italian Americans in organized crime, have influenced the public's inaccurate and negative perception of this ethnic group. This exaggeration can be seen in the suggestion that Italian Americans developed organized crime in the United States and that a significant percentage of Italian Americans are involved in the Mafia.[6]

Unfortunately, due to the negative portrayal of Italian Americans, a self-fulfilling prophecy begins to develop within their own group. This can be seen in Zogby International's *National Survey: American Teenagers and Stereotyping* which reveals that teens learn the less admirable aspects of their heritage from entertainment industry stereotyping. The Report indicates that 46 percent of Italian American teens said that television's portrayal of Italian Americans as crime bosses is accurate and 30 percent said that they were proud of their TV image. Moreover, the Report shows that 78 percent of all American teenagers associate Italian Americans with criminal activities.[7] In addition, another study revealed that a significant percent of all Americans in all age groups feel that all Italian Americans are connected to the mob.[8]

These recent studies indicate that Italian Americans are still portrayed and perceived as being involved in criminality and socially undesirable behavior. Moreover, these studies show that many Americans believe Italian Americans developed organized crime in the United States and that a significant percentage of Italian Americans are involved in the Mafia. However, social scientific studies do not support these commonly held beliefs about Italian Americans. This chapter will now present a more accurate representation of Italian Americans.

First, research points out that Italian Americans did not develop organized crime in the United States. H. Abadinsky's book *Organized Crime* (1985) points out that organized crime existed in the United States before the arrival of the large numbers of Italian immigrants from 1880 to 1920. This study discusses the negative practices by such famous nineteenth century businessmen as John Jacob Astor, Cornelius Vanderbilt, John D. Rockefeller, and others. Such practices included extortion, blackmail, violence, bribery, murder, and the use of thugs and private armies to destroy a competitor. This work verifies that the practices of the nineteenth century businessmen were no different from the practices of Italian American gangsters of the twentieth century. Moreover, the book indicates that the social, economic, historical and cultural conditions in the United States produced organized crime.[9]

Second, D. Cauchon's article "Head of BCCI-linked Bank Quits,"[10] A. Block and F. Scarpitti's book *Poisoning for Profit: The Mafia and Toxic Waste*[11] and W. Chambliss' study *On the Take: From Petty Crooks to Presidents*[12] detail the huge involvement of the police, big businesses, and the CIA in the development of organized crime groups. In addition, J. Mills' book *The Underground Empire: Where Crime and Government Embrace* presents evidence revealing that the United States government has been a major player in international drug crime systems.[13] These works show the role that the government (including the CIA and the police) and big business have played in the growth of organized crime in the U.S.

Third, V. Kappeler, M. Blumberg, and G. Potter's book *The Mythology of Crime and Criminal Justice* describes the prevalent practices employed by the media, law enforcement personnel, and government officials to manipulate information and create crime myths. Some of these practices involve creating criminal stereotypes, interjecting personal opinion into media presentation without factual basis; presenting certain facts and not others; and presenting supposedly factual information with undocumented sources of authority. Their work indicates that the media, law enforcement personnel and government officials have used such practices to blame Italian Americans for developing organized crime. Furthermore, Kappeler, Blumberg, and Potter's book convincingly argues that the socioeconomic conditions of American society need to be investigated in order to understand the cause of organized crime.[14]

Data indicate that contrary to popular belief a significant percentage of Italian Americans are not involved in the Mafia. As a matter of fact, only a fraction of 1 percent of all Italian Americans participate in organized crime.[15]

According to the Federal Bureau of Investigation, there were allegedly 5,000 Italian American who were made members of the Mafia at the height of involvement. Currently, according to the FBI, there are 1,500 Italian Americans who are members of the Mafia out of 20 million Italian Americans. Furthermore, of an estimated 500,000 members of organized crime in America today, Italian Americans make up a slim 0.3 percent of all involved.[16]

In short, the evidence demonstrates that the widely held beliefs about Italians are unfounded. Italian Americans did not develop organized crime in the United States and only a fraction of a percent of all Italian

Americans participates in organized crime. In addition, social scientific research points out social, economic, historical and cultural factors of American society gave rise to organized crime. This is something that needs to be addressed and studied further in order to prevent future increases in crime rates while increasing our standard of living.

The reasons, according to this author, for blaming Italian Americans for organized crime are as follows. First, the media finds Italian American organized crime stories profitable. Second, some politicians, especially when their opponent is Italian American, find associating Italian Americans with organized crime useful for winning votes.

It is this author's opinion that as long as the above and widely held belief about Italian Americans and organized crime continues to exist in the United States, organized crime will not be dealt with properly. Kappeler, Blumberg, and Potter's *The Mythology of Crime and Criminal Justice* indicates that the media, law enforcement personnel and the U.S. government need to be held accountable for the blaming of a single ethnic group for the development of organized crime in the United States.[17] Moreover, law enforcement agencies, big businesses and the government need to take responsibility for their part in participating in many organized activities. For instance, David R. Simon's book *Elite Deviance* examines the institutionalized set of deviant practices by elites (persons from the highest strata of U.S. society) that are international. His book points out these elites' collaboration with organized crime involved in the 850 billion dollar global narcotics trade and the vast amount of money laundered by legitimate financial institutions, lawyers and other elite professionals.[18]

To deal with organized crime more successfully according to this author, it makes sense to think of organized crime as a business that provides illegal goods and services, rather than an Italian or alien conspiracy. It needs to be recognized that organized crime is able to flourish primarily because of the high demand for goods and services (for instance, drugs) that have been designated as illegal.

Moreover, efforts need to focus on identifying and dealing with political, corporate and financial deviance that serves as links between the underworld and upper world. For example, Stephen M. Rossoff, Henry W. Pontell and Robert Tillman's book *Profit without Honor: White Collar Crime and the Looting of America* points out that corrupt banks are central to the operations of organized crime that import billions of dollars of illegal drugs into the U.S.[19]

In conclusion, recent studies indicate that Italian Americans are inaccurately portrayed and misperceived as being involved in criminality and socially undesirable behavior. Moreover, research shows organized crime is able to flourish primarily because of the high demand for goods and services that have been designated as illegal and not because it is an Italian or alien conspiracy.

Finally, this chapter makes the following recommendations, based on R. A. Capozzola's *Finalmente: The Truth about Organized Crime)* [20] and Carol Chiago Lujinnos' study "The Only Real Indian is the Stereotyped Indian," [21] to deal with the incorrect, negative representations and misunderstanding of Italian Americans, as previously stated. First, more Italian Americans need to support and participate in such organizations as the Order Sons of Italy in America, the National Italian American Foundation and Unico National. Second, more Italian Americans need to voice their protests, concerns, or objections by phoning or writing to radio stations, television networks, newspapers, and magazines that offend their group as well as other groups. Third, more Italian Americans need to hold accountable politicians, actors, celebrities, and writers who portraying Italian Americans, as well as other groups, falsely and negatively. Fourth, more Italian Americans need to boycott movies, TV shows, products and businesses that offend their group as well as other groups. Fifth, more Italian Americans need to speak up when someone is saying something that is inaccurate and offensive about their group and about other groups. Sixth, long-term efforts to reduce negative stereotyping of Italian Americans include establishing and supporting Italian American studies programs at both state and privately funded educational institutions. Seventh, books and other publications in law, government, history, and the social sciences need to include a more widespread analysis of the Italian American experience. Eighth, Italian Americans need to become more noticeable and concerned in politics, law and education, as well as in other leadership ranks, to support a more truthful representation of Italian Americans.

NOTES

1. This chapter is an updated version of a chapter that was published in Louis Gesualdi, *The Italian American Experience: A Collection of Writings* (Lanham, Maryland: University Press of America, 2012).

2. S. Robert Lichter and Daniel R. Amundon, *Portrayal of Italian American Character in Prime Television Series, 1994–1995,* Washington, DC: Social Justice Order Sons of Italy, 1996.

3. Bill Dal Cerro, *Italian Culture on Film, 1928–1999,* Floral Park, NY: Italic Studies Institute Image Research Project, 1999.

4. Janice Therese Mancuso, "Searching for Italian American History" (paper) presented at the American
Italian Sociohistorical Association First Conference Series entitled *The Italian American Experience: A Sociohistorical Examination* held at St. John's University, Queens, NY, October 21, 2015. Also, see Italic Institute of America, "Film Study 2015 (1914–2014)," italic.org/media watch/filmstudy.php, 2015, and Italic Institute of America, "Exhibit A: Examples of Media Bias,"italic.org/anti_defamation/ExhibitA.php., 2015.

5. *Americans of Italian Decent: A Study of Public Images, Beliefs and Misperceptions,* Washington, DC: The National Public Opinion Research Commission for Social Justice Order Sons of Italy, 1991.

6. Richard A. Capozzola, *Finalmente: The Truth about Organized Crime,* Altamonte Springs, FL: Five Centuries Books, 2001.

7. Zogby International, *National Survey: American Teenagers and Stereotyping,* Utica, NY: Zogby International, 2001.

8. See M. Alfano, "Negative Stereotype Persist though FBI Figures Reveal Facts," *ComUnico Magazine,* April 2002.

9. Howard Abadinsky, *Organized Crime,* Chicago, IL: Nelson Hall, 1985.

10. D. Cauchon, "Head of BCCI-Link Bank Quits," *USA Today,* August 15, 1991.

11. A. Block and F. Scarpitti, *Poisoning for Profit: The Mafia and Toxic Waste,* New York: William Morrow, 1985.

12. William Chambliss, *On the Take: From Petty Crooks to Presidents,* Bloomington: Indiana University Press, 1978.

13. J. Mills, *The Underground Empire: Where Crime and Government Embrace,* New York: Doubleday, 1986.

14. Victor Kappeler, Mark Blumberg and Gary Potter, *The Mythology of Crime and Criminal Justice,* Illinois: Waveland Press, 2000.

15. Richard Gambino, "America's Most Tolerated Intolerance: Bigotry against Italian Americans," *The Italian American Review* (Spring/Summer) 1997.

16. M. Alfano, "Negative Stereotype Persist though FBI Figures Reveal Facts," *ComUnico Magazine,* April 2002.

17. Victor Kappeler, Mark Blumberg and Gary Potter, *The Mythology of Crime and Criminal Justice,* Illinois: Waveland Press, 2000.

18. D. R. Simon, *Elite Deviance,* Boston: Allyn and Bacon, 1999.

19. Stephen M. Rossoff, Henry W. Pontell and Robert H. Tillman, *Profit without Honor: White-Collar Crime and the Looting of America,* New Jersey: Pearson Education, Inc., 2002.

20. Richard A. Capozzola, *Finalmente: The Truth about Organized Crime,* Altamonte Springs, FL: Five Centuries Books, 2001.

21. Carol Chiago Lujinnos, "The Only Real Indian is the Stereotyped Indian" in Coramae Richey Mann and Marjorie S. Zatz (eds.) *Images of Color Images of Crime,* CA: Roxbury Publishing Co., 1998.

NINE

A Brief Critique on the 2015 PBS Special on Italian Americans

Lisa Kuan and Louis J. Gesualdi

This chapter presents a brief critique on the 2015 PBS special on Italian Americans.[1] It needs to be stated that the individual testimonial experiences, presented by the PBS special, were very good. However the special had too many weaknesses and limitations. Before we begin on critiquing the Italian American Experience, we would first like to discuss how damaging stereotypes and discrimination can be and we can use this information in our own analysis of the 2015 PBS special on Italian Americans.

Ray C. Rist's "Student Social Class and Teacher Expectations: The Self-fulfilling Prophecy in Ghetto Education" shows how the perception of teachers can lead to a life of unbalanced resources as early on as kindergarten. These perceptions are derived from the images that the teacher considers to be of middle class standards and ranges from the parent's socioeconomic status, the type of language students use, clothing, scent, and other subjective analysis. This is before any abilities or examinations of the students were measured and taken into consideration, and therefore, was all based on a teacher's perspectives. After the teacher groups the students by using his or her own perspectives, assigned seats and tables were given to students and here begins the uneven distribution of help and attention. The children from the top table then harassed other students in the lower tables and belittled them and called the other students names. The teacher's first impression of the students now became a self-fulfilling prophecy and will be confirmed through exams throughout the later grades.[2]

Rist's results of his study is also the case with Jennie Oakes in *Keeping Track*. Oakes found that even when African Americans and Latinos scored the same in national math exams, they were less likely to be in college prep classes when compared to Asians and whites. Again, one can see that perceptions and stereotypes play a large role in a person's life.[3]

However, Jeffrey M.R. Duncan-Andrade in his article "Note to educators: Hope Required When Growing Roses in Concrete" calls for educators to stop giving students false hope and to stop delegitimizing their legitimate feelings and sufferings. He believes that teachers should stop giving students the illusion that everything is fair and equal because it is not.[4] This can clearly be seen in the PBS special "The Italian American Experience."

First, only 4 hours was dedicated to the 120 years of the Italian American experience. A thorough documentary would have provided at least 12 hours of the Italian American experience or one hour per decade. Furthermore, a significant part of the documentary's 4 hours was spent on the Italian Americans in the entertainment industry. A history of Italian Americans in entertainment and pop culture could have been a separate PBS special.

The entertainment and pop culture section the PBS special made no reference to the cinematic history of portraying Italian Americans negatively. Bill Dal Cerro's research show since 1928, a consistently negative portrayal of Italian Americans occurred 74 percent of the time. Of all the movies dealing with Italian Americans, images of Italian Americans as violent criminals predominates (41 percent), followed by portrayals of boors, buffoons, bigots and other social undesirables (33 percent). The figures (quantitative data) clearly indicate an entrenched, institutionalized bias against Americans of Italian descent in the entertainment industry.[5] The few films that portrayed Italian Americans in a positive way include "From Here to Eternity," "Marty," "Serpico," "Brian's Song," "Unbroken" and the independent film "Matewan" which were not mentioned in the PBS special.

PBS did not discuss the padrone system of 1890 to 1930. A significant percentage of Italian immigrants (numbering thousands of thousands) at the time worked under this slave-like condition. In many cases, these immigrants worked in mines, railroads, agribusiness and quarries for companies under extremely harsh and unsanitary conditions.[6] Nor did it mention that perhaps as many as 1.5 million Italian Americans served in World War II for the United States. Italian Americans probably made up 10 percent of the United States military during WWII.[7] The special was also lacking in presenting other quantitative research which shows that only a fraction of 1 percent of all Italian Americans participates in organized crime. For instance, according to the Federal Bureau of Investigation, there were allegedly 5,000 Italian Americans who were members of organized crime at the height of their involvement. Currently there are 1,500 Italian Americans who are members of organized crime out of 20 million Italian Americans. Furthermore, of an estimated 500,000 members of organized crime in America today, Italian Americans make up a slim 0.3 percent of all involved.[8] These data were not presented in the special.

The PBS special ironically did not present important individuals in Italian American studies. Such individuals include Giovanni Schiavo, John N. LaCorte and Salvatore LaGumina.

Giovanni Schiavo is known as the father of Italian American studies. Schiavo had devoted and dedicated sixty years of his life to researching and publishing works on the Italian American experience. His books involve the following: *The Italians in America before the Civil War; Italian American History, Vol. I; Italian American History, Vol. II; Four Centuries of Italian–American History; The Truth about the Mafia and Organized Crime;* and *The Italians in America before the Revolution.*[9]

John N. LaCorte is founder of the Italian Historical Society and worked for the awareness and recognition of such Italian Americans as Meucci—inventor of the telephone, Bonaparte—first head of the FBI, and Verrazano—the great navigator and others.[10]

Salvatore LaGumina is currently a historian of Italian American Studies (author and editor of approximately 20 books on the Italian American Experience) and one of the founders of the American Italian Historical Association. Such books include *The Humble and the Heroic: Wartime Italian Americans; WOP! A Documentary History of Anti-Discrimination; Long Island Italians: History, Heritage and Tradition; Hollywood's Italians: From Periphery to Prominent* and others books.[11]

Individuals who also needed to be discussed in the PBS special were Frank Cavaioli, Richard Gambino, Joseph Lopreato, Jerome Krase, Richard Juliani, Virginia Yans-McLaughlin, Luciano Iorizzo, Silvano Tomasi, Lydio Tomasi, Betty Boyd Caroli, Jean Scarpaci, Elizabeth Messina, Paola Sensi-Isola and among others.[12] There exist almost a hundred years of Italian American scholars involved in Italian American Studies. Unfortunately, one would not have gotten that impression by watching the PBS schedule.

The PBS special also did not present and discuss a history of different Italian American organizations that were set up in response to the discrimination against Italian Americans. Such organizations include the thousands of mutual benefit societies throughout the United States which were established by Italian immigrants.[13] Other organizations include the Sons of Italy, Unico, the American Italian Historical Association and the John D. Calandra Institute.

The PBS special did not discuss Italian Americans as an affirmative action group at CUNY (the City University of New York) for the past 30 years. Italian Americans as an affirmative action at CUNY are underrepresented as full time professors at CUNY. It also did not indicate that students of Italian descent at CUNY are considered an affirmative action group. The special also did not discuss individuals (Joseph Scelsa and Vincenzo Milione) and their research that indicated discrimination against Italian Americans at CUNY.[14]

In Episode Four: The American Dream (1945 to present day) although the "Italian American Experience" provides the achievements of Mario Cuomo and Nancy Pelosi, and Antonin Scalia, there was a complete disregard of Italian Americans in academia and the sciences. Walter Marty Schirra Jr. or "Wally" was one of the many individuals that were not mentioned. The only astronaut who flew in the Mercury, Gemini and Apollo programs should have been mentioned.[15]

Enrico Fermi was another scientist who was not mentioned. He received the Nobel Prize in Physics for his work on artificial radioactivity produced by neutrons and for nuclear reactions brought about by slow neutrons. Some of his other works consist of research on general relativity and quantum mechanics; he also built a prototype of the first nuclear reactor (Chicago Pile 1), and worked on the Manhattan Project.[16]

Anthony S. Fauci is another scientist, an immunologist who has made significant contributions in the study of immunodeficiency including HIV/AIDS. Fauci is currently the director of the National Institute of Allergy and Infectious Diseases.[17]

And there is the ISSNAF, the Italian Scientist and Scholars of North America Foundation. This organization as its name describes, was established in 2008 by 36 prominent Italian scientists in North America; among the founders of this organization were 4 Nobel Prize laureates.[18]

In conclusion, discrimination can affect the entire life of an individual and can begin as early on as kindergarten or pre-school. Therefore, it is important that we analyze what is shown in the media, especially from such a trusted institution such as PBS. This paper's response to the PBS special on the Italian American Experience criticizes its presentation of Italian Americans on two general counts. First, there were insufficiencies in the special's description of Italian Americans living in the United States during the last 120 years and second, there were weaknesses in its analysis of the true Italian American experience. Disappointedly, this PBS special failed significantly in showing the many great achievements of Italian American scholars, including the significant contributions in science. By omitting all these great scholars, this special unfortunately portrays the image that there are no scholars of Italian American descent. We hope to have shown that this is not the case. It is as if PBS wanted to perpetuate institutionalized discrimination by omission for Italian Americans.

NOTES

1. This chapter was originally presented by Lisa Kuan and Louis Gesualdi "A Brief Critique on the PBS Special on the Italian American Experience" (paper) at the *Italian American Experience: A Sociohistorical Examination* (American Italian Sociohistorical Association First Conference Series, October 21, 2015).

2. Ray C. Rist, "Student Social Class and Teacher Expectations: The Self-fulfilling Prophecy in Ghetto Education," *Harvard Education Review*, Vol. 40, No. 3, (August 1970).

3. Jeannie Oakes, *Keeping Track: How Schools Structure Inequality* (New Haven, CT: Yale University Press, 2005).

4. Jeffrey M. R, Duncan-Andrade, "Note to Educators: Hope Required When Growing Roses in Concrete" *Harvard Educational Review*, Volume 79, Number 2 (Summer 2009).

5. Bill Dal Cerro, *Italian Culture on Film 1928–1999* (Floral Park, NY: Italic Studies Institute Research Project, 1999).

6. Richard Alba, *Italian Americans into the Twilight of Ethnicity* (Englewood Cliffs, New Jersey: Prentice Hall, 1985).

7. See Peter L. Belmonte, *Italian-Americans in World War II*. Illinois: Arcadia Publishing. 2001and Eric Martone, *Italian Americans: The History and Culture of a People* (Santa Barbara, California: ABC-CLIO, December 12, 2016).

8. M. Alfano, "Negative Stereotype Persist through FBI Figures Reveal Facts," *ComUnico Magazine*, (April, 2002).

9. See Gesualdi, L. *The Italian American Experience: A Collection of Writings* (Lanham, Maryland: University Press of America, 2012), 35–36.

10. See John N. LaCorte Bio- Italian Historical Society, www.italianhistorical.org .

11. See Salvatore LaGumina Collection, Stony Brook University Special Collections and University Archives, www.stonybrook.edu and Salvatore J. LaGumina Books, biblio.com.

12. See American Italian Historical Association Publication of Proceedings, Staten Island, NY: American Italian Historical Association, 1968–2005, Joseph Lopreato, *Italian Americans* (New York: Random House, 1970), and Richard Gambino, *Blood of My Blood: The Dilemma of the Italian-Americans* (Garden City, NY: Anchor Press/Doubleday, 1974).

13. Nathan Glazer and Daniel P. Moynihan, *Beyond the Melting Pot* (Cambridge Massachusetts: The M.I.T. Press, 1970), 194.

14. See Joseph Scelsa, "Remarks Made as Keynote Speaker" at the *Italian Americans and Discrimination in Higher Education Conference* held at St. John's University, Queens, NY, March 27, 2013 and "Remarks Made as Morning Speaker" at the *Italian American Experience: A Sociohistorical Examination* (American Italian Sociohistorical Association First Conference Series, October 21, 2015). Also see, Vincenzo Milione, "Italian American Workforce and Labor Pool Changes" (paper presented at the *Italian Americans and Discrimination in Higher Education Conference* held at St. John's University, March 27, 2013).

15. See Elizabeth Howell, "Wally Schirra: Mercury, Gemini and Apollo Astronaut" in www.space.com, October 16, 2018 and Wally Schirra Home Page and About Wally Page, www.wallyschirra.com.

16. See Enrico Fermi- Biographical - www.nobelprize.org .

17. See Anthony S. Fauci, M.D., NIAID Director, www.niad.nih.gov .

18. See Italian Scientist and Scholars of North America Foundation, www.issnaf.org.

TEN

Criticisms of the Banning of Columbus Day

Francis N. Elmi and Louis J. Gesualdi

On February 2, 2016, Brown University faculty officially changed "Fall Weekend," formerly known as Columbus Day, to "Indigenous People's Day." A group of Native Americans created a student-led campaign to change Columbus Day to "Fall Weekend" in 2009, thus erasing any respect for Columbus's heroic explorations without which the Americas would not have developed into havens for immigration from Europe and Asia. But that was not enough for Brown University. A petition was then signed by over 1,100 students, faculty, staff, and alumni leading to the change from "Fall Weekend" to "Indigenous' People's Day."[1] The petition reads in part:

> We are formally requesting that the university vote to make this change to promote the on-campus visibility of the resistance and resilience of Native peoples and Native students on Brown's campus against the continued attempts at disempowerment, disenfranchisement, erasure, and genocide that began with the arrival of Christopher Columbus.[2]

Can we really blame over 525 years of disempowerment, disenfranchisement, erasure, and genocide on the arrival of Christopher Columbus? Is that logical? Is that true? Are these champions of the name-change thinking clearly? Do they really believe that one man so long ago is responsible for all of today's problems that Native Americans are encountering?

This paper will explore these questions as we seek to confront the erasure of Columbus at such a distinguished institution at Brown University, one of America's renowned Ivy League universities. The following comprise our criticisms of Brown University banning Columbus Day.

- Brown University's referring to the first peoples (Native Americans) here in the Americas as "indigenous' peoples" is inaccurate. It needs to be stated that the term indigenous peoples does not apply to Native Americans. There are no indigenous peoples in the Americas. There are first peoples in the Americas. The only continent with indigenous peoples is Africa. No humans evolved in the Americas. The Native Americans migrated here from Asia. They were the first peoples here in the Americas.

- Brown University prefers to believe that Columbus's discoveries led to genocide against the New World's peaceful Native Americans, and uniformly vilifies him—as if he had orchestrated these atrocities himself or as if the Native American tribes had not already been waging war on one another.[3]

- Columbus has been defamed in a thoughtless and extreme manner. Judging someone from the 1490s by today's standards is really quite illogical and stupid. Ernle Bradford's biography, *Christopher Columbus,* as long ago as 1973 stated: "It is easy enough some five hundred years later to criticize Columbus and his methods—and those of the Spaniards who followed him—but it is essential to try and understand the thinking of his time. The promulgation of an assertive Christianity was bred in their bones, and especially in Mediterranean men who had suffered so much from Mohammedanism. The whole of life, as they saw it, was a battle between the Cross and the Crescent. It was all-important that any foreign people whom they encountered should be converted in order to add to the weight of the armies that fought for the "true religion."[4] Even in 2019 we are having similar religious battles. Is Columbus responsible for them as well?

- Columbus has become the scapegoat for all the evils that have engulfed Native Americans of the Americas. The Americas have been presented as a paradise before Columbus. This is not accurate. There were violent tribes of Native Americans throughout the Americas before Columbus. Human sacrifice, cannibalism (for instance, the Carib tribe) and abandonment of the sick and the elderly were not uncommon in the Americas by Native Americans before Columbus. Also, the Aztecs and Incas had empires no different from empires in Europe, Africa or—complete with imperialism, slavery, genocide, rape and exploitation.[5]

By defaming Columbus, Brown University fails to acknowledge the exploitation, ethnocentrism and stereotyping of today's Native Americans in the United States. The following are some examples of the exploitation, ethnocentrism and stereotyping of today's Native Americans in the United States.[6]

- Contemporary Native Americans often are stereotyped as backward, unmotivated, continually drunk, or are regarded as romantic anachronisms.
- Many frequently over generalize about Native Americans, seeing the many tribes as one people even though the tribes have always differed from one another in language, social structure, values and practices.
- Today, many people in the US are oblivious to Native Americans' problems and consider them quaint relics of the past; others find them undesirable and some want their land and will use almost any means to secure it.
- Native Americans still encounter discrimination in stores, bars, and housing, particularly in cities and near the reservations. They have been beaten or killed and their property rights infringed on.
- Of all the minorities in the United States, according to government statistics on income, Native Americans are the "poorest of the poor."
- Encroachment on Native American land continues. Water and energy needs have led government and industry to look covetously at reservation land once considered worthless.
- Poor, but with large tracts of isolated land, Native Americans in recent years have seen their reservations recommended as toxic-waste dumping grounds.
- Urban sprawl and agribusiness have led to the sinking of deep wells around reservations in Arizona, siphoning off the water reserves of several tribes.
- A growing number of sacred Native American sites are under threat from housing developments and industrial plants.[7]

Any reasonable person can see that the above problems that today's Native Americans in the U.S. are experiencing have nothing to do with Columbus. One can argue that the problems that today's Native Americans in the U.S. are experiencing are outcomes of a market economy.[8] Also, it needs to be stated that Brown University in its banning of Columbus Day chose to ignore the worldly contributions of Christopher Columbus. The following is a listing of the contributions of Columbus:

- Great navigation skills were developed under Columbus to sail the Atlantic Ocean. Columbus had an amazing understanding of winds. He used known islands off of Africa as a springboard to the Indies and sailed a northern voyage to return.[9]
- Columbus opened up a new world to Europeans, Africans and Asians.[10]

- A widespread transfer of animals, plants, microbes, culture and human population developed as a result of Columbus's voyages.[11]
- Food (such as, corn, potatoes, tomatoes, peanuts, etc.) was sent from the Americas to Europe (as well as all over the world). This helped end famine in Europe.[12]
- Indigenous peoples benefited from iron tools, firearms, horses, and farm animals brought by the Europeans. Overall, the movement of humans, animals, plants and technology ultimately benefited humankind.[13]
- Columbus's voyages represent globalization, multiculturalism and the expansion of human knowledge.[14]

In conclusion, the petition of over 1,100 students, faculty, staff, and alumni of Brown University misleads the American people about Columbus and denies the long term positives that Columbus' voyages brought humanity. Perhaps, Brown University should have acted on changing the University's name since the Brown family, founders of Brown University and Brown's University's namesake family, were slaveholders and profited from the slave trade along with members of the Brown University Board during the University's early years.[15] It is also to be noted that Columbus never stepped foot on land comprising the current United States. The Native Americans in what is now the United States of America suffered discrimination, violence, and genocide as a result of the activities of English settlers, their descendants, and the Manifest Destiny of creating a nation to expand economic and political power on the North American continent.[16]

NOTES

1. Brown's University, "Indigenous' People's Day," February 2, 2016, brown-university-indigenous-peoples-day and see Sean Spears, "Brown University Change, Name of Fall Weekend to Indigenous People's Day," *USA Today*, February 3, 2016 and Daniel Victor, At Brown University, Columbus Day is Now Indigenous People's Day," *New York Times*, February 3, 2016.

2. Ibid.

3. See Italic Institute of America, *Why Columbus Day* (brochure), 2015, www.italic.org and Martin Dugard, *The Last Voyage of Columbus*. New York: Little Brown and Company, 2005.

4. Ernle Bradford, *Christopher Columbus*. New York: Viking Press, 1973.

5. See Italic Institute of America, *Why Columbus Day* (brochure), 2015, www.italic.org and Martin Dugard, *The Last Voyage of Columbus*. New York: Little Brown and Company, 2005.

6. See Vincent Parrillo, *Strangers to These Shores*, New Jersey: Pearson, 2003: chapter 4.

7. Ibid.

8. See Louis Gesualdi, *A Peacemaking Approach to Criminology*. New York: University Press of America, 2014.

9. Italic Institute of America, *Why Columbus Day* (brochure), 2015, www.italic.org .

10. Ibid.

11. Ibid.

12. ack Weatherford, *Indian Givers*, New York: Random House, 2010.

13. Italic Institute of America, *Why Columbus Day* (brochure), 2015, www.italic.org .

14. See Jack Weatherford, *Indian Givers*, New York: Random House, 2010 and Italic Institute of America, *Why Columbus Day* (brochure), 2015, www.italic.org .

15. See Craig Wilder, *Ebony and Ivy: Race, Slavery and the Troubled History of American Universities*, New York: Bloomsbury, 2013.

16. Michael Giammarella, "Re: Holiday name change." Message to Mark Nickel at Brown University's Office of Public Relations. 15 Feb. 2016. E-mail and Vincent Parrillo, *Strangers to These Shores*, New Jersey: Pearson, 2003, chapters 4 and 10.

ELEVEN

Some Ideas for Research and Projects for the American Italian Sociohistorical Association

Louis J. Gesualdi and Lisa Kuan

A large amount of research has been done on Italian Americans throughout the twentieth century. However, continued research and projects, in particular quantitative research, is still needed to better understand the Italian American experience. The newly formed American Italian Sociohistorical Association can focus on the following ideas for research and projects. It should be stated that some of the following ideas can overlap with each other. Furthermore, it should be stated that we are open to any suggestions you may have dealing with Italian American studies.

IDEAS FOR RESEARCH

- Italian American relationship with Asian Americans, African Americans and Latino Americans

A very high percentage of studies involved the Italian American relationship with Irish Americans. The American Italian Historical Association has had conferences concerning the Italian American relationship with Irish Americans, Jewish Americans and African Americans. Research is needed dealing with the relationship of Italian Americans with Asian American and Latino American experiences. Many Italian American neighborhoods have been in close proximity to Asian, African and Latino American neighborhoods. It is important to study the conflict and cooperation that exist/existed among these groups. Also, this research would include an examination of intermarriage between Italian Americans and the following: Asian Americans and/or African Americans and/or Latino Americans.

- Occupational and educational achievements of Italian American Research on occupational and educational attainments of Italian Americans is continual research. That is, this type of research needs to be done on a regular basis in order to understand the development of Italian Americans in the United States.
- The Development of the Italian Americans and the Italians in Italy Research is needed to discuss the international quantitative social science research on the emigration and immigration of Italians and the compatible contemporary development of the Italian Americans in the United States and Italians in Italy. This type of research needs to be done on a regular basis in order to understand the development of Italian Americans in the United States and the Italians in Italy. Also, such quantitative social science research is needed to examine the development of Italian Americans in Canada and in countries in South America, as well as people of Italian ancestry in Australia and in other countries.
- The Italian American suburbs
- A majority of studies deal with Italian Americans in the cities. A very large percentage of Italian Americans live in the suburbs. It is important to examine which cultural traits are maintained by Italian Americans in suburbia and which ones disappear? Which ethnic groups do Italian Americans tend to live with in the suburbs and why?
- The Italian/American experience in industry, education, politics, religion, sciences and the arts

This research needs to be done on a regular basis in order to a complete understanding of the Italian American experience. False perceptions of Italian Americans still persist by the American public (for instance, many Americans view Italian Americans in general as gangsters and/or buffoons). Continued research on the Italian American experience in industry, education, politics, religion, sciences and the arts may help dispel such false perceptions.

- Prejudice and discrimination toward Italian Americans

Prejudice and discrimination have existed and still exist against Italian Americans. For instance, some studies indicate that many Americans still associate Italian Americans with organized crime (even though, only a fraction of one percent of all Italian Americans are involved in organized crime). More research is needed to document a history of prejudice and discrimination against Italian Americans and also is needed to examine any prejudice and discrimination that exist today.

- Experience of Italian American women

Although there are some studies of the experiences of Italian American women, more studies are needed. This has been a largely neglected subject of research.

- Ideas for Projects for the American Italian Sociohistorical Association

The American Italian Sociohistorical Association (AISA) needs to continue to have conferences on the Italian American experience not only in Italy but in different countries. The dissemination of information on the Italian American experience all over the world would be an excellent mission for the AISA.

- The proceedings of all AISA conferences need to be published. The publications of the proceedings will be referred to as the John N. LaCorte Topical Issues Series (named in honor and memory of John N. LaCorte for his work on the Italian American experience).
- The AISA needs to set up a website to disseminate information on the Italian American experience.
- The AISA needs to have conferences by way of the internet and to have the proceedings of these conferences published online in a series to possibly be referred to as the Antonio Meucci Internet Conference Series (named in honor and memory of Antonio Meucci, the true inventor of the telephone).
- The AISA needs to produce on DVD ½ hour and 1-hour documentaries and also produce documentary series on the Italian American experience. These documentaries will not only be shown at conferences but possibly on PBS stations, the American History Channel, and Public Access Stations. Also, these documentaries can be placed on YouTube and/or on an AISA website.
- AISA needs to include the Italian American experience in modern times in order to examine the development of different generations of Italian Americans and to showcase their contributions to American culture. This includes contributions to science, engineering, technology, education and the government, just to name a few areas of influence. Showcasing their contributions will help fight against traditional Italian stereotypes.
- Finally, the AISA needs to disseminate information by way of publishing monographs on the Italian Americans experience in a series to possibly be referred to as the Four Navigators da Italia Monograph Series (named in honor and memory of four great navigators from Italy—Christopher Columbus, John Cabot, Amerigo Vespucci and Giovanni Verrazano).

In conclusion, it is important that Italian Americans (as well as other ethnic groups) are familiar with their own group's experience and to grasp what is considered productive and practical to shaping their lives. Some of the ideas for research and projects to be done by the American Sociohistorical Association that were presented in this chapter may be useful for Italian Americans to become aware of their positive history.

Bibliography

Abadinsky, Howard. *Organized Crime*, Chicago, IL: Nelson Hall, 1985.

Alba, Richard D. *Italian Americans into the Twilight of Ethnicity*, Englewood Cliffs, New Jersey: Prentice-Hall, Inc., 1985.

Alfano, M. "Negative Stereotype Persist though FBI Figures Reveal Facts," *ComUnico Magazine*, April 2002.

American Civil Liberties Union. *The Constitution of the United States of America*, New York: American Civil Liberties Union.

American Italian Historical Association Publication of Proceedings, Staten Island, NY: American Italian Historical Association, 1968–2005.

Americans of Italian Decent: A Study of Public Images, Beliefs and Misperceptions, Washington, DC: The National Public Opinion Research Commission for Social Justice Order Sons of Italy, 1991.

Anthony S. Fauci, M.D., NIAID Director, www.niad.nih.gov.

Austin, Algernon. "African Americans Are Still Concentrated in Neighborhoods with High Poverty and Still Lack Full Access to Decent Housing," in www.epi.org/publications/african-americans-concentrated-neighborhoods .

Barcella, Michael. *Italactors 101 Years of Italian Americans in U.S. Entertainment*, Washington, DC: National Italian American Foundation, 2000.

Barclay, Hartley W. *Civil War in Hersheytown*," published in *Mill and Factory*, Qtd. In Lola Romanucci-Ross. *To Love the Stranger: The Making of an Anthropologist*, North Charleston: Create Space Platform, 2012. Also Qtd. In Samuel N. Tancredi, Oral History Interview with Samuel N. Tancredi, Hershey, PA: Hershey Community Archives Oral History Collection, 900H18, 30 July 1990.

Barzini, Luigi. *The Italians: A Full-Length Portrait Featuring Their Manners and Morals*. New York: Atheneum, 1964.

Beccaria, Cesare. *An Essay on Crimes and Punishments*, Wellesley, MA: International Pocket Library, 1983.

Belmonte, Peter L. *Italian-Americans in World War II*. Illinois: Arcadia Publishing. 2001.

Bettina, Elizabeth. *It Happened in Italy: Untold Stories of How the People Defied the Horrors of The Holocaust*, Nashville, TN: Thomas Nelson Publishers, 2011.

Blakemore, Eric. "Why America Targeted Italian Americans during World War II," History.com, January 19, 2019.

Block, A. and Scarpitti, F. *Poisoning for Profit: The Mafia and Toxic Waste*, New York: William Morrow, 1985.

Bosworth, R.J.B. *Mussolini*. New York: Oxford University Press, 2002.

Bradford, Ernle. *Christopher Columbus*. New York: Viking Press, 1973.

Brodsky, Alyn. *The Great Mayor: Fiorello LaGuardia and the Making of the City of New York*, New York: Truman Talley Books, 2003

Brooks, David. "The Ideology of Hate and How to Fight It." —*The New York Times* 6 August 2019: A 19.

Brown's University. "Indigenous' People's Day," February 2, 2016, Brown-university-indigenous-peoples-day.

Bruhn, John G. and Wolf, Steward. *The Roseto Story: An Anatomy of Health*, (Norman, Oklahoma: University of Oklahoma Press, 1979).

Burnim, Mellonee V. and Maultsby, Portia K. (editors), *African American Music: An Introduction* (second edition), New York: Taylor and Francis, 2015.

Burrow, Gerard N. A History *of Yale's School of Medicine: Passing Torches to Others,* New Haven, CT: Yale University Press, 2002.

Capozzola. Richard A. *Finalmente: The Truth about Organized Crime,* Altamonte Springs, FL: Five Centuries Books, 2001.

Cauchon, D. "Head of BCCI-Link Bank Quits," *USA Today,* August 15, 1991.

Celata, Giuseppe. *The Jews of Pitigliano: Four Centuries of a Diverse Community.* Pitigliano, Grosseto, Italy: n. p. Printed by A.T.L.A. 2015.

Chambliss, William. *On the Take: From Petty Crooks to Presidents,* Bloomington: Indiana University Press, 1978.

Clough, Shepard B. and Saladino, Salvatore. *A History of Modern Italy: Documents, Reading, and Commentary.* New York: Columbia University Press, 1968.

Cole, Nicki Lisa. "11 Black Scholars and Intellectuals Who Influenced Sociology" in thoughtco.com, July 3, 2019.

Dawidowicz, Lucy. *The War against the Jews, 193 –1945,* New York: Holt, Rinehart and Winston, 1975.

D'Antonio, Michael. *Hershey: Milton S. Hershey's Extraordinary Life of Wealth, Empire, and Utopian Dreams.* New York: Simon and Schuster, 2006.

Dal Cerro, Bill. *Italian Culture on Film, 1928–1999,* Floral Park, NY: Italic Studies Institute Image Research Project, 1999.

Dekle, Natalie Mykta. *Building a New Life: The Italian Community in Hershey.* Hershey, PA: Italian Lodge, 1990.

Duffy, Eamon. *Saints and Sinners: A History of Popes.* New Haven: Yale UP, 1997.

Dugard, Martin. *The Last Voyage of Columbus.* New York: Little Brown and Company, 2005.

Duggan, Christopher. *The Force of Destiny, a History of Italy since 1796.* New York: Houghton Mifflin, 2008.

Duncan-Andrade, Jeffrey M.R. "Note to Educators: Hope Required When Growing Roses in Concrete" *Harvard Educational Review,* Volume 79, Number 2 (Summer 2009).

Elmi, Francis. Rosemary Elmi Interview. June 4, 2015.

Elmi, Francis. Alvesta Tancredi Interview. June 4, 2015.

Enrico Fermi- Biographical—www.nobelprize.org.

50 African Americans Who Forever Changed Academia—OnlineCollege.

Formiconi Giuseppe and Dreassi, Mario. *Pitigliano: Guida Turistica.* Translated by Gina Macchiarulo Elmi, Pitigliano, GR: Consiglio di Amministrazione Della Cassa Rurale Ed Artigiano di Pitigliano, A.T.L.A., 1985.

Gambino, Richard. "America's Most Tolerated Intolerance: Bigotry against Italian Americans," *The Italian American Review* (Spring/Summer) 1997.

Gambino, Richard. *Blood of My Blood: The Dilemma of the Italian-Americans,* New York: Doubleday, 1974.

Gesualdi, Louis. *The Bad Things You Have Heard About Italian Americans Are Wrong: Essays on Popular Prejudice,* Lewiston, NY: The Edwin Mellen Press, 2014.

Gesualdi, Louis. *A Peacemaking Approach to Criminology.* New York: University Press of America, 2014

Gesualdi, Louis. *The Italian/American Experience: A Collection of Writings,* Lanham, Maryland: University Press of America, 2012.

Gesualdi, Louis. *The Italian Immigrants of Connecticut, 1880 to 1940,* New Haven, Connecticut: Connecticut Academy of Arts and Sciences, 1997.

Gesualdi, Louis and Kuan, Lisa. "Cesare Beccaria's *On Crime and Punishment: A Preliminary Report"* presented at the *Over Five Centuries of Italian American History* (American Italian Sociohistorical Association Third Conference Series held at the University of Cork, Cork, Ireland, July 28, 2017).

Gesualdi, Louis and Kuan, Lisa. "The Holocaust and Italy: A Preliminary Report" at the *Over Five Centuries of Italian American History,* the American Italian Sociohistorical Association Third Conference Series held at the University of Cork, Cork, Ireland (July 28, 2017).

Giammarella, Michael. "Re: Holiday name change." Message to Mark Nickel at Brown University's Office of Public Relations. 15 Feb. 2016. E-mail.

Giustizia e Liberta, no.1, November 1929; AGL, sezione IV, fascicolo 2, sotto fascicolo 1, insert 2, no. 1.

Glazer, Nathan and Moynihan, Daniel P. *Beyond the Melting Pot,* Cambridge, Massachusetts: The M.I.T. Press, 1970.

Hapsburg-Lorraine. Pietro Leopoldo. Qtd. in *Pitigliano: Guida Turistica.* Giuseppe Formiconi and Mauro Dreassi. Translated by Gina Macchiarulo Elmi, Pitigliano GR: Consiglio di Amministrazione Della Cassa Rurale Ed Artigiano di Pitigliano, A.T.L.A., 1985.

Hartensian, Larry. *Benito Mussolini.* New York: Chelsea House Publishers, 1988.

Hershey Community Archives Oral History Collection, Hershey, PA, 1998.

Hohn, Maria. "African American GIs of WWII: Fighting for Democracy Abroad and at Home," *Black Military History* in *Military Times,* militarytimes.com, January 30, 2018.

Howell, Elizabeth. "Wally Schirra: Mercury, Gemini and Apollo Astronaut" in www. space.com , October 16, 2018.

Italian Americans ONE VOICE Coalition Supports Court Petition to Have Italian Americans Included in CUNY Affirmative Action Plan, May 25, 2018, iaovc.org.

Italian Scientist and Scholars of North America Foundation, www.issnaf.org.

Italic Institute of America. *Why Columbus Day* (Brochure), 2015, www.italic.org .

Italic Institute of America. "Exhibit A: Examples of Media Bias," Italic.org/ anti_defamation/ExhibitA.php., 2015.

Italic Institute of America. "Film Study 2015 (1914–2014)," italic.org/mediawatch/film-study.php, 2015.

Janken, Kenneth R. "The Civil Rights Movement 1919–1960s, Freedom's Story, TeacherServe. National Humanities Center. December 29, 2019. http://nationalhumaniescenter.org/tserve/freedom/1917beyond/essays/crm.htm.

John N. LaCorte Bio- Italian Historical Society, www.italianhistorical.org.

Jones, Tobias. *The Dark Heart of Italy.* New York: North Point Press. A division of Farrar, Straus, and Giroux, 2003.

Kappeler, Victor, Blumberg, Mark and Potter, Gary. *The Mythology of Crime and Criminal Justice,* Illinois: Waveland Press, 2000.

Kuan, Lisa and Gesualdi, Louis. "A Brief Critique on the PBS Special on the Italian American Experience" (paper) presented at the *Italian American Experience: A Sociohistorical Examination* (American Italian Sociohistorical Association First Conference Series, October 21, 2015).

Leonardi, Carmela. "AIAE Association of Italian American Educators 20 years of Dedication to The Promotion of Italian Language and Culture" (presentation) at the American Sociohistorical Second St. Joseph's Day Celebration Program Conference Series held at St. John's University, Queens, NY, April 4, 2017.

Levi-Montalcini, Rita. *In Praise of Imperfection: My Life and Work,* Trans. Luigi Attardi. New York: Basic Books Inc., 1988.

Lichter, S. Robert and Amundon, Daniel R. *Portrayal of Italian American Character in Prime Television Series, 1994–1995,* Washington, D.C.: Social Justice Order Sons of Italy, 1996.

Lopreato, Joseph. *Italian Americans* (New York: Random House, 1970)

Loser, Mathew. Oral History Interview with Angelo Elmi. Hershey, PA: Hershey Community Archives Oral History Collection, 980H101, 1/27/1998 and 2/ 20 1998.

Loser, Mathew. Oral History Interview with Edward C. Tancredi. Hershey, PA: Hershey Community Archives Oral History Collection, 910H27, 8/11/1991.

Luria, Salvador Edward. *A Slot Machine, A Broken Test Tube,* New York: Harper and Row Publishers, 1984.

Lujinnos, Carol Chiago. "The Only Real Indian is the Stereotyped Indian" in Coramae Richey Mann and Marjorie S. Zatz (eds.) Images of Color Images of Crime, CA: Roxbury Publishing Co., 1998.

Machlin, Edda Servi. *The Classic Cuisine of the Italian Jews: Traditional Recipes and Menus and a Memoir of a Vanished Way of Life*, New York: Dodd, Mead and Company, Inc. 1981.

Maestro, Marcello, T. *Cesare Beccaria and the Origins of Penal Reform*. Philadelphia, PA: Temple University Press, 1973.

Maestro, Marcello T. *Voltaire and Beccaria as Reformers of Criminal Law*. New York: Columbia University Press, 1942.

Mahoney, Thomas T. "African Americans in the Twentieth Century." EH.Net Encyclopedia, edited by Robert Whaples. January 14, 2002.

Mancuso, Janice Therese. "Searching for Italian American History" (paper) presented at the American Italian Sociohistorical Association First Conference Series entitled *The Italian American Experience: A Sociohistorical Examination* held at St. John's University Queens, NY, October 21, 2015.

Martone, Eric. *Italian Americans: The History and Culture of a People* (Santa Barbara, California: ABC-CLIO, December 12, 2016).

McMahon, James D. *Built on Chocolate: The Story of the Hershey Chocolate Company*. Santa Monica: General Publishing Group, Inc., Hershey Foods Corporation, 1998.

Meyer, Gerald. *Vito Marcantonio: Radical Politician 1902–1954*, Albany, NY: State University of New York Press, 1989.

Milione, Vincenzo. (Presentation) "Italian American Workforce and Labor Pool Changes" at the Italian Americans and Discrimination in Higher Education Conference held at St. John's University, Queens, NY, March 27, 2013.

Mills, J. *The Underground Empire: Where Crime and Government Embrace*, New York: Doubleday, 1986.

Monachesi, Elio D. "Cesare Beccaria," Journal of Criminal Law, Criminology and Political Science 46: 439–49.

Moore, Christopher Paul. *Fighting for America: Black Soldiers—The Unsung Heroes of World War II*, New York: The Random House Publishing Group, 2005.

Moorhead, Caroline. *A Bold and Dangerous Family*. New York: Harper Collins Publishers, 2017.

Morgagni Medical Society of New York, About Us Page, Morgagnimedicalsociety.com.

Murray, Emily Grace. "100 Years of Memories: A Personal History of Vae (Alvesta) Tancredi." *Reflections: The Newsletter of the Hershey-Derry Township Historical Society*, vol. 22, no. 2, 2015, pp. 3–6.

Murray, Emily Grace. "100 Years of Memories: A Personal History of Vae (Alvesta) Tancredi." *Reflections: The Newsletter of the Hershey-Derry Township Historical Society*, vol. 21, no. 4, 2014, pp. 3–5.

National Italian American Sports Hall of Fame - www.niashf.org .

New York Post (front cover). August 14, 2019.

Oakes, Jeanine. *Keeping Track: How Schools Structure Inequality* (New Haven, CT: Yale University Press, 2005).

Okrent, Daniel. *The Guarded Gate: Bigotry, Eugenics, and the Law That Kept Two Generations of Jews, Italians, and Other Europeans Out of America*. New York: Scribner, 2019.

Order of Sons and Daughters of Italy in America, About Us—osia.org.

Paioletti, Louis. Re: *Building a New Life: The Italian Community in Hershey* by Natalie Dekle. "Message to Francis N. Elmi." 21 May 2015.

Parrillo, Vincent. *Strangers to These Shores*, New Jersey: Pearson, 2003.

Phillipson, Coleman. *Three Criminal Law Reformers: Beccaria, Bentham and Romilly*. Montclair, NJ: Patterson Smith, 1923.

Piceno, Ascoli. *The New Encyclopedia Britannica Micropaedia*, edited by the faculties of the University of Chicago, 15th edition, vol. 1, The University of Chicago, 1977.

Pugliese, Stanislao. *Carlo Rosselli: Socialist Heretic and Antifascist Exile*. Cambridge: Harvard University Press, 1999.

Rist, Ray C. "Student Social Class and Teacher Expectations: The Self-fulfilling prophecy in Ghetto Education," *Harvard Education Review*, Vol. 40, No. 3, (August 1970).

Romanucci-Ross, Lola. *To Love the Stranger: The Making of an Anthropologist:* North Charleston: Create Space Independent Publishing Platform, 2012.

Romanucci-Ross, Lola. *One Hundred Towers: An Italian Odyssey of Cultural Survival* New York: Begin and Garvey, 1991.

Rossoff, Stephen M, Pontell, Henry W. and Tillman, Robert H. *Profit without Honor: White-Collar Crime and the Looting of America,* New Jersey: Pearson Education, Inc., 2002.

Salvatore LaGumina Collection, Stony Brook University Special Collections and University Archives, www.stonybrook.edu.

Salvatore J. LaGumina Books, biblio.com.

Scelsa, Joseph. "Remarks Made as Morning Speaker" at the *Italian American Experience: A Sociohistorical Examination* (American Italian Sociohistorical Association First Conference Series, October 21, 2015).

Scelsa, Joseph. "Remarks Made as Keynote Speaker" at the *Italian Americans and Discrimination in Higher Education Conference* held at St. John's University, Queens, NY, March 27, 2013.

Scelsa, Joseph. "Italian Americans as an Affirmative Action Category at CUNY," paper presented at the *Italian Americans and Discrimination in Higher Education Conference* held at St. John's University, Queens, NY, 2013.

Schwartz, David N. *The Last Man Who Knew Everything: The Life and Times of Enrico Fermi, Father of the Nuclear Age.* New York: Basic Books, 2017.

Segre, Gino and Hoerlin, Bettina. *The Pope of Physics: Fermi and the Birth of the Atomic Age.* New York: Picador Henry Holt and Company, 2016.

Servi Machlin, Edda. *The Classic Cuisine of the Italian Jews: Traditional Recipes and a Memoir of a Vanished Way of Life.* New York: Dodd, Mead and Company, Inc., 1981.

Simon, D. R. *Elite Deviance,* Boston: Allyn and Bacon, 1999.

Smith, Denis Mack. *Modern Italy: A Political History.* Ann Arbor: The University of Michigan Press, 1997.

Smith, Tom. *The Crescent City Lynchings: The Murder of Chief Hennessy, the New Orleans "Mafia" Trials, and the Parish Prison Mob,* Guilford, CT: The Lyons Press, 2007.

Sopranos TV Series 1999-2007- IMDb.

Southern Poverty Law Center. About Us, http://www.splcenter.org.

Spears, Sean. "Brown University Change, Name of Fall Weekend to Indigenous People's Day," *USA Today,* February 3, 2016.

Stave, Bruce M. and Sutherland, John F. with Salerno, Aldo. *From the Old Country: An Oral History of European Migration to America,* New York: Twayne Publishers, 1994.

Steinberg, Stephen. *Turning Back: The Retreat from Racial Justice.* Boston, MA: Beacon Press, 1995.

2018 Movie—"The Green Book."

2015 PBS Special on Italian Americans.

2020 "The Many Saints of Newark," MOVIEWEB.

UNICO National. About UNICO—www.unico.org.

Victor, Daniel. At Brown University, Columbus Day is Now Indigenous People's Day," *New York Times,* February 3, 2016.

Vigliotti, Cynthia L., Vivo, Gianna, Attardo, Salvatore and Brown-Clark, Sarah. "Stereotyping Ethnicity: The Ideology of Film Representations of Italian Americans and African Americans" in Dan Ashyk, Fred L. Gardaphe and Anthony Julian Tamburri, *Shades of Black and White: Conflict and Collaboration between Two Communities,* Staten Island, NY: American Italian Historical Association, 1999.

Wallace, Paul A.W. and Shippen, Katherine B. *Milton S. Hershey.* From *Biography of Milton S. Hershey.* New York: Random House, 1959.

Wally Schirra Home Page and About Wally Page, www.wallyschirra.com.

Weatherford, Jack. *Indian Givers,* New York: Random House, 2010.

Well-Barnett, Ida B. *On Lynchings.* Mineola, NY: Dover Publications, 2014.

Whitlock, Catherine and Evans, Rhodri. *10 Women Who Changed Science and the World.* New York: Diversion Books, 2019.

Whitman, Walt. "By Blue Ontario's Shore." *Walt Whitman: The Complete Poems.* Edited by Francis Murphy. New York: Penguin Group USA, 364–365.

Wiggins, David K. *More Than a Game: A History of the African American Experience in Sport,* New York: Rowman and Littlefield, 2018.

Wilder, Craig. *Ebony and Ivy: Race, Slavery and the Troubled History of American Universities,* New York: Bloomsbury, 2013.

Williams III, Frank P. and McShane, Marilyn D. *Criminological Theory,* Englewood Cliffs, NJ: Prentice Hall, 1988.

Williams, Richard. Oral History Interview with Samuel N. Tancredi. Hershey, PA: Hershey Community Archives Oral History Collection, 900H18, 30 7, 1990.

Witter, Brad. "Martin Luther King Jr. and 8 Black Activists Who Led the Civil Rights Movement," *Biography* in biography.com, June 24, 2019.

Wolff, Walter. *Bad Times Good People: A Holocaust Survivor Recounts His Life in Italy during WWII,* Long Beach, NY: Whittier, 1998.

Zogby International, *National Survey: American Teenagers and Stereotyping,* Utica, NY: Zogby International, 2001.

Index

About the Authors

Francis N. Elmi is a Professor Emeritus, in English, at the City University of New York. A native of Hershey, Pennsylvania, Dr. Elmi's family originated in Tuscany, Puglia, and Sicily, as well as New York, and he has a special interest in Italian American Studies. He has also taught at the Pennsylvania State University, Albright College, and Harrisburg Community College in Pennsylvania as well as at Pratt Institute, the College of New Rochelle, and LaGuardia Community College in New York. He has a Ph.D. in Higher Education from New York University with a concentration in sociology and an internship in counseling at Pace University. He also has an M.A. in English from the Pennsylvania State University. Dr. Elmi has co-written and is the editor of Student Survival Guide, a textbook specifically for an orientation course at The Borough of Manhattan Community College of the City University of New York which went into a second edition. He also published "Yamanaka and Faulkner: Teaching the New Canon with the Old" in Inquirer, a journal about teaching and learning and "The Integration of Counseling, Academic Advisement, and Academic Mission in a Community College" which appeared in Community Review, Journal for College Faculty in Two-Year Degree Program as well as co-authoring Italian-Americans: The Neglected Minority in City University: A Call for Affirmative Action! In his CUNY Calandra Institute Fellowship, Dr. Elmi wrote an in-house report: "The Invisible Minority: A History of the Italian American Struggle for Justice and Equality at The City University of New York."

Louis J. Gesualdi is Professor of Sociology at the Lesley H. and William L. Collins College of Professional Studies, St. John's University. He received his Ph.D. in sociology from Fordham University in 1988. He has published the following books, *The Italian Immigrants in Connecticut, 1880–1940, The Italian/American Experience: A Collection of Writings, A Peacemaking Approach to Criminology: A Collection of Writings, The Bad Things You Have Heard about Italian Americans Are Wrong: Essays on Popular Prejudice,* and *A Source Book of Karl Marx's Letters about Abraham Lincoln and His Strategic Goal in the Civil War: The Destratification of American Society.*

Lisa Kuan was a Research Associate/Lab Manager for the New York University Langone Medical Center—Microbiology from January, 2012 to September, 2014. Ms. Kuan has two research articles published in the area of Biology with a concentration in recombinant DNA technology. Lisa Kuan received her MS in Biology with a concentration in recombinant DNA technology at New York University. She received her Masters of Science degree in Adolescent Education in Biology at St. John's University.